Laura De

G. R. A. C. E.

[Gospel Reform And Covenant Evangelism]

presents

Rearing Faithful Children

A Biblical Handbook for Child Discipline

by

Craig Mutton

INFINITY
PUBLISHING

ISBN 0-7414-1642-5

Published by:

PUBLISHING.COM

519 West Lancaster Avenue
Haverford, PA 19041-1413
Info@buybooksontheweb.com
www.buybooksontheweb.com
Toll-free (877) BUY BOOK
Local Phone (610) 520-2500
Fax (610) 519-0261

Printed in the United States of America

Printed on Recycled Paper

Published August 2003

Dedication

I dedicate this book to my father, Frank Mutton, and to the memory of my mother, Lillian (Weber) Mutton.

May their children's children's children rise up and call them blessed.

Author's Foreword:

G. R. A. C. E.
[Gospel Reform And Covenant Evangelism]

Gospel Reform And Covenant Evangelism is the name the author gives to his personal ministry. It springs from the concept that true reform, whether personal, organizational or societal, can only come from the "new man" in Christ Jesus. The Gospel changes men at the core, which provides the foundation for change at other levels. To assist in the reform process, we preach the Gospel in a Covenant context.

God relates to His people in terms of His Covenant. When we evangelize, we bring people into a covenant relationship with God through Jesus Christ. That Covenant embraces all facets of human life. Therefore, the reform begun by the Gospel in a sinner's heart continues as the new believer learns to live [by grace] in compliance with the Covenant.

This book is one in a proposed series of books dealing with life in the Covenant. I have tried to structure the books to serve the needs of both believers and unbelievers. Each book will begin with a presentation of the Gospel, so that it can be used as an evangelistic tool, while the body of the book serves as instruction in one aspect of Covenant living.

For further inquiry into **G.R.A.C.E.** Ministries, or to arrange for the author to speak to your group, contact:

G.R.A.C.E. Ministries
102 West Chapman Road
Belton, SC 29627

Table of Contents

Contents   Page number

Dedication

Author's Foreword

Preface: The Gospel 1

Introduction: Rearing Children in the Covenant 11

Part One: God Determines the Agenda

Chapter One: Where Do Babies Come From? 17

Part Two: God Appoints Parents as His Agents

Chapter Two: Life in the Covenant with Father: 24

Chapter Three: Reap Huge Profits 49

Part Three: God Sets the Standards

Chapter Four: Truth in Labeling 62

Chapter Five: Strive Toward the Goal 77

Chapter Six: A Doctrine of Discipline 85

Part Four: God Prescribes Life-Changing Discipline

Chapter Seven: Giving Godly Spankings 97

Chapter Eight: Is It Ever Too Late? 119

Part Five: Only God's Grace Guarantees the Result

Chapter Nine: Discipling for Destiny 131

Appendix: 150

The Gospel of The Kingdom of The Lord Jesus Christ

1. God Exists: Those Who Reject God Acknowledge Him Even In Their Rejection

Do you believe in God? When I ask you if you believe in God, I do not mean just any god. I do not mean a vague higher power, an impersonal force, destiny or some more highly evolved order of being. When I ask if you believe in the existence of God, I want to know if you believe in the God described in the Bible - the God of Christianity. He is specifically the personal (Father, Son, Holy Spirit), infinite, all powerful Spirit who created the heavens and the earth out of nothing. He depends on nothing outside Himself, but every other thing depends upon Him for its existence. Do you believe in that God?

If you can acknowledge the existence of the God I have just described, you may want to continue on to the next section of this tract, entitled "Purpose". If, on the other hand, you do not acknowledge God's existence, I have an important principle to convey to you. The principle is both profound and profoundly simple. It states: **Whatever reason you advance against God's existence constitutes the most solid proof that He does exist.** Although you may think the statement preposterous, I hope you will read on so that I can explain to you what I mean.

First, let us back up a little to contrast the basic views of the universe necessary to atheism and to Christianity. The atheist believes the universe "just is" with no intelligent design or reason behind it - reality is ultimately non-rational. The Christian sees the universe

1

as ultimately rational -- the product of God's intelligent, purposeful, creative act. In other words, the atheistic belief system rests upon ultimate nonreason, while Christianity looks to ultimate reason to explain the world around us. This places the nonbeliever on the horns of a dilemma.

When the Christian believer appeals to reason, he does so in perfect accord with his basic assertion that reason -- God's reason -- lies behind everything. When the nonbeliever trys to use reason or logic to disprove God, however, his faith in ultimate nonreason leaves him no basis on which to justify his use of reason. He is trying to use reason to prove ultimate nonreason. But by acknowledging reason, he is denying what he is trying to prove (nonreason). To say this another way, the nonchristian must borrow something (reason) from the Christian's worldview in order to argue against Christianity's God. Therefore, **any and every reason you may try to use against God's existence actually testifies to the fact that He exists.**

Whether someone claims to hold to atheism or not, he and you and I have all resisted God in some fashion. The Bible tells us we do so because of an inborn bias against God, called sin. You can find out about the origin of that bias in the next segment.

2. Purpose: God Created Mankind as a Race of Kings and Queens

One of the great nagging questions of life appears as some form of, "Why am I here?" "Does my existence have a purpose?" "Do I have a destiny?" A look into the Bible will reveal the answer to these questions by leading us to the works of God Himself.

At the creation of man and woman the Lord God declared man's function and purpose. He said,

> Let Us make man in Our image, according to Our likeness; let them have dominion over the fish of the sea, over the birds of the air, and over the cattle, over all the earth, and over every creeping thing that creeps on the earth. (Genesis 1: 26)

God created mankind in His image, then He appointed them to rule over all else He had made. He originally fashioned us as a race of kings and queens, His royal representatives over the rest of creation (Genesis 1:28).

Had not a drastic change taken place at that early point of history, the landscape today might take the form of a series of park-like gardens, each one ruled over by a husband and wife serving as vice-regents of the King of Heaven. The change came over the issue of who would determine the laws that should govern the newly created earth. The Lord had placed man in the garden to cultivate it and keep (or guard) it (Genesis 2:15), and in addition He gave man specific instructions not to eat of a particular tree that represented the knowledge of good and evil (Genesis 2:16-17). In other words, God reserved for Himself the authority to determine what constitutes right and wrong in the world He had made. Man would acknowledge this as God's domain alone by not eating from that particular tree. But then a problem arose.

3

A trespasser entered the garden -- the tempter who came in the form of a serpent. He challenged the heavenly King's decree regarding the tree. Mankind could, at this point, have ejected the serpent from the garden under the authority that God gave him to guard the garden. Instead, the man and woman ate and became rebels against their God and King. Moreover, they voluntarily placed themselves and their offspring under the rule of the tempter, Satan. Since that time human beings have entered the world as sinners and subjects of the kingdom of Darkness.

Each of us has exercised his will to confirm that act of rebellion in the garden. Even though we utterly depend on God -- even for the mind and will we have used to reject Him -- we show our bias against God as we try to live our lives independent of Him. Regardless of our respective stations in life, each of us stands before the High King of Heaven as a rebel. From the beginning of rebellion, though, God gave mankind hope in the form of a promise.

In His word of judgment on the serpent the LORD said,
> *I will put enmity between you and the woman, and between your seed and her seed; He shall bruise your head, and you shall bruise His heel (Genesis 3:15).*

The progressive expansion and fulfillment of that promised Seed makes up the bulk of the Bible record. You can read about some of the highlights under the next heading, "Promise".

3. Promise: At Various Times and in Different Ways God Told That a Ruler Would Come to Undo the Disaster of Sin.

The King of Heaven spoke not only to Adam and Eve, but also to and through men like Noah, Abraham, Moses, David and the prophets. He told them of One Who would come to redeem men from their sin (their inborn bias against God), and Who would restore the holy reign of God in human hearts and throughout the earth.

One of the clearest prophecies of redemption came through Isaiah the Prophet, who recorded the following about God's sin-bearing Servant:

He is despised and rejected by men,

A Man of sorrows and acquainted with grief,

And we hid, as it were, our faces from Him;

He was despised and we did not esteem Him.

Surely He has borne our griefs

And carried our sorrows;

Yet we esteemed Him stricken,

Smitten by God and afflicted.

But He was wounded for our transgressions,

He was bruised for our iniquities;

The chastisement of our peace was upon Him,

And by His stripes we are healed.

All we like sheep have gone astray,

We have turned every one to his own way;

And the LORD has laid on Him the iniquity of us all. (Isaiah 53:3-6)

The Lord gave the prophet Daniel a clear vision of the Coming One as Ruler over an everlasting kingdom. Daniel wrote:

I was watching in the night visions,

And behold One like the Son of Man,

Coming on the clouds of heaven.

He came to the Ancient of Days,

And they brought Him near before Him.

Then to Him was given dominion and glory and a kingdom,

That all peoples, nations, and languages should serve Him.

His dominion is an everlasting dominion,

Which shall not pass away,

And His kingdom the one

Which shall not be destroyed. (Daniel 7: 13-14)

Jesus, in fact, began His public preaching with a quote from one of the prophecies about the Kingdom of God:

And He was handed the book of the prophet Isaiah, and when He had opened the book, He found the place where it was written: "The Spirit of the LORD is upon Me,

Because He has anointed Me to preach the gospel to the poor.

He has sent Me to heal the brokenhearted,

To preach deliverance to the captives

And recovery of sight to the blind,

To set at liberty those who are oppressed,

To preach the acceptable year of the LORD."

Then He closed the book and gave it back to the attendant and sat down. And the eyes of all who were in the synagogue were fixed on Him. And He began to say to them, "Today this Scripture is fulfilled in your hearing." (Luke 4: 17-21, see Isaiah 61: 1-2)

As you can see, the Lord Jesus Christ came to fulfill God's promises of a Redeemer/King. You can read about His ministry under the heading "Presentation" on the next page.

6

4. Presentation: Jesus Came to Fulfill God's Promises

The Lord Jesus Christ came as God's Anointed One (Christ means *messiah* or *anointed*). God anointed Jesus as the ultimate Prophet, Priest and King. From His miraculous conception and birth to His proclamation of the Kingdom of God which were accompanied by a host of supernatural signs -- from His death for sinners to His glorious resurrection and ascension into the presence of His eternal Father, the life of Christ demonstrates His goodness, His power and His authority. **He is Lord of all**.

He turned water into wine, multiplied a few loaves of bread to feed a multitude and walked upon the surface of a storm-tossed sea. He showed His compassion when He healed the sick, restored sight to the blind, made the lame to walk and raised the dead. He assaulted the strongholds of the evil realm as He cast out demons and restored the victims of the Dark Lord to their right minds. As He spoke to the heart of the multitude, He spoke words of comfort, words of grace and healing, and words that called men to change their hearts and lives. He astonished His hearers, "for He taught them as one having authority and not as the scribes" (Matthew 7:29). After He rose from the dead He proclaimed to His disciples, "All authority has been given to Me in heaven and on earth" (Matthew 28:19).

The Apostle John described Him as "Jesus Christ, the faithful witness, the firstborn from the dead, and the ruler over the kings of the earth" (Revelation 1:5). Peter and the other apostles made a similar declaration when the rulers in Jerusalem issued an edict that directly contradicted a command they had received from the risen Christ. They said, "God has exalted [Jesus] to His right hand to be Prince and Savior, to give repentance to Israel and forgiveness of sins" (Acts 5:31). On another occasion Peter had preached, "God has made this Jesus...both Lord and Christ" (Acts 2:36). He well knew when he said it that the title **Lord** held particular significance in the Roman Empire.

The Apostle Paul wrote to certain subjects of Rome, "God has highly exalted Him [Jesus] and given Him the name which is above every name, that at the name of Jesus every knee should bow of those in heaven, and of those on earth and of those under the earth, and that every tongue should confess that Jesus Christ is Lord, to the glory of God the Father" (Philippians 2: 9-11). Paul's bold words flew in the face of Roman imperial tradition, for the emperor required his subjects to acknowledge him as the supreme authority in all matters by means of an oath that simply stated, "Caesar is Lord." The apostles, on the other hand, set forth Jesus' claim to exercise authority over all kings, potentates, presidents and premiers. In order for the apostles to consider someone a Christian, that person would have to confess, "Jesus is Lord."

> . . . that if you confess with your mouth Jesus as Lord and believe in your heart that God has raised Him from the dead, you will be saved. For with the heart one believes to righteousness and with the mouth confession is made to salvation. (Romans 10: 9-10)

Upon confession of Jesus as Lord, the Church baptized the new citizen of the Kingdom along with his children and admitted them to the communion table.

When the Church has taken the meaning of that confession seriously, and when earthly powers have recognized its import, bloody persecutions of the heavenly King's subjects have often followed.

Is Jesus your Lord and Savior? The next section -- "Proclamation -- tells you more about it.

8

5. Proclamation: God Demands Unconditional Surrender

[N]ow God commands all men everywhere to repent. (Acts 17: 30)

The Lord God sent His Son **to redeem a people and to rule over all the world.** To all of us -- who are born in the realm of darkness, -- He issues the command to abandon our willful resistance and give full allegiance to the One Who is King over all Kings. The Bible informs us that the two elements of repentance and faith form the core of this new allegiance.

When we freely admit that God has been right all along, and that we have been wrong, we stand at the threshold of repentance. Repentance recognizes that the Divine King has the rightful authority to determine the basis for all our thoughts, opinions, decisions, desires and actions. His authority over our lives transcends that of any human governor, president or king, so that if any earthly authority clashes with His rule, we owe Him first loyalty and obedience (*We ought to obey God rather than men* Acts 5:29). [*]

Although even a mature and seasoned disciple of the Lord Jesus will not have every aspect of his life in full submission at any given time, he fully acknowledges Christ's rightful claim to his full compliance, and he hates any remnants of disloyalty or disobedience which he finds within. This is strong evidence of true repentance.

---

[*] For the sake of peace the Heavenly King bids us render obedience to earthly rulers unless they explicitly command us contrary to the ordinances of God (Romans 13: 1-7; I Peter 2: 13-17).

The term faith, as used in the Bible, encompasses two important concepts. First, faith takes God at His word. In other words to have faith in the Lord Jesus means that we simply accept the truth of what God says about Him in the Bible. We believe that He came into the world born of a virgin, lived a holy and sinless life, healed the sick, performed miracles, died for the sins of His people, rose up from the grave and now reigns from heaven at the right hand of God the Father. Beyond that, Biblical faith also means something very close to the idea of faithfulness, a *pledge of faith*.

In other words, for the Christian disciple his ultimate pledge of allegiance is not to a flag or a country, but to Christ, God's Prophet, Priest and High King over all creation.

Why should you repent and put your faith in Jesus the Christ? Some preachers try to induce a "commitment" on the basis of the hope of heaven or the threat of hell or the promise of emotional benefits, etc. In the final analysis, however, the gospel message does not center on us and how we do or do not benefit.

God in His grace has given His people forgiveness and pardon from sin, the promise of life forever in heaven with Him and grace to face the trials of this life, and we ought to show our gratitude for His might and mercy. However, the plain fact as stated in Scripture remains: *now God **commands** all men everywhere to repent (Acts 17:30)*. In the final analysis, no one can provide a better reason for following the Lord Jesus than that the Almighty Ruler of heaven and earth demands it.

Introduction:

Rearing Children in the Covenant

1. You, Me and This Book

My motivation for writing *Rearing Faithful Children* came from my desire to pass on to my children and my grandchildren what I have learned from the Bible about bringing up children to be faithful to Christ. I wanted to be able to put in their hands the general rules and practical tips that God has funneled to me directly -- through His Word -- as well as indirectly -- through the lives and words of others. Secondarily, but quite consciously I wrote this as a handbook of discipline for all those Christian parents who seek direction in bringing their children up in the faith. If you fall into this category, you are sharing in the most precious legacy that I pass on to my heirs.

You may have picked up this copy of *Rearing Faithful Children* as a parent or grandparent, but you do not have the kind of relationship with the Lord Jesus such as I describe in the preface. If that's the case, then this volume will bring limited benefit to you. I invite you, however, to return to the preface and deliver yourself in total surrender to the King of Kings, so that you can start living your life in His Kingdom and in terms of His covenant. At that point, this book will have relevance as instruction in one aspect of covenant living.

As I have said, this book is for Christian parents. But I did not write it as a comprehensive reference on parenting. You won't find these pages brimming with practical tips on breast feeding, teething, or toilet train-ing. I have tried to maintain my focus on one major theme, and that is how to train up your children in such a way that they will follow in the faith of their fathers.

2. The Thesis of This Book

The Bible tells us that the marriage of believers establishes a covenant household (Malachi 3:14). The Bible also teaches that God established the marriage covenant to raise up godly offspring (Malachi 3:15, *et. al.*). God alone changes the hearts of children to make them faithful to Him. He does, however, delegate certain vital responsibilities to the parents[1].

The major thesis of this book is that the guarantee of a covenant child's salvation turns upon faithful parental discipline. That is to say, a parent who faithfully applies the Biblical precepts regarding parental discipline of a covenant child has a promise that God will save that child. The Christian parent who does not apply Scriptural discipline has no such promise from God (*i.e.,* his child may or may not grow up to become a Christian). I expect this thesis to arouse some controversy among those who may read this book.

I have tried to lay the Biblical foundation for the book's thesis in its first chapters. I have also tried to anticipate and answer major objections to the book's argument. Nevertheless, there will be those who strongly oppose the message I have set forth. I simply ask you, the reader, to consider the evidence and to draw a prayerful, thoughtful conclusion. Of course I hope you will, in the end, agree with me.

If, however, you reject my central message, I hope you will still find the practical applications useful and an encouragement to you as you endeavor to bring up

---

[1]See Chapter Two, **Life in the Covenant with Father.**

12

your children in the nurture and admonition of the Lord.

3. The Structure of This Book

Those of you familiar with the five-point structure of Biblical covenants will recognize that I have organized the chapters of *Rearing Faithful Children* loosely along those lines. I have done so, because as Christians we must realize that God's covenant extends to every corner of our lives and encompasses every facet of our being. The God of the covenant is the God who made us. Therefore, the issues we confront in His covenant are the issues we must face in every relationship we have, including our relationship to our children.

Here are the covenantal truths around which I have organized this material:

1. God Determines the Agenda. As the Sovereign of Heaven, God takes the initiative in seeking and saving the lost. He forges His covenant with His people. He sets the terms of the covenant, and He fulfills His covenant promises.

Since the children of Christians are children of the covenant, God determines the agenda for them and their parents. We can't negotiate special terms for our situation.

2. God Appoints Parents as His Agents. God has his covenantal representatives in the Church and in the state. Parents -- especially fathers -- represent God in the home. They lead the little ones to Him in prayer. Parents are the channel through which God supplies His little children with daily bread. They also act in His name and authority when they mete out discipline.

God has given us certain promises concerning our (actually, *His*) children -- and marvelous promises they are. He has also determined the conditions on which He will fulfill those promises -- and our duty is to meet those conditions.

3. God Sets the Standard for Life and Discipline. Many parents have dreams for their children's vocational paths. These may vary, but for Christian parents the objective and standard for their children's growth remains constant because God gives us the standard for Christian maturity in His Word.

As we seek to mold the conduct and the character of our offspring, we must look to Scripture as the only source for our standards. God has told us in His book what He expects us to be and how He expects us to act. He also lays down the precepts on which we must base our discipline.

4. God Prescribes Life-Changing Discipline. By precept and example God has laid down not only the theory but also the practice that will discipline children to obedience. Actually, it's the same method that He has used in your life and mine to train us to godliness. I have tried to explain both the theory as well as the practice of Biblical child-discipline, so that you may apply it to your own children.

5. God's Grace Alone Guarantees the Results. I mentioned above that God makes certain covenant promises, and that we must meet certain conditions in order to see those promises fulfilled. As you will see in chapter two, this is true with regard to your children and their eternal future. However, both you and I must guard against the prideful error that the

14

fulfillment of the covenant rests in any way upon our works. If you do well with your children, don't pat yourself on the back. Rather you should kneel in thanksgiving before Him for continuing the good work which He began in you, and which He will bring to completion in the day of Christ.

Disclaimer:

This book addresses the subject of child discipline, including spanking. All that is said about the subject assumes that the child is a normal, healthy child, without any conditions which might result in life-or-health-threatening complications. It is the parent's responsibility to get medical confirmation of the child's general health and fitness. The author assumes no liability for misapplication of the techniques described herein, and makes no recommendation about their suitability for use with specific children and/or specific health conditions.

Nothing I have written in this book (or anywhere else) should be construed to advocate any manner of child punishment more severe than the use of a thin, light rod on the child's buttocks with only such force as will cause no serious or lasting injury.

Punching, kicking, biting, or the shaking of a child are totally inappropriate, as are striking the child's face, twisting its limbs, the use of sharp or jagged objects, or the use of boiling water or hot objects to burn a child. These and other injurious practices are signs of an adult out of control. If you or anyone you are acquainted with has ever done any of these things, please seek counsel from a pastor qualified in the field of Nouthetic Counseling. For more information about Nouthetic (*i.e.,* Biblical Counseling), contact:

Christian Counseling & Educational Foundation
1803 E. Willow Grove Ave., Glenside PA, 19038
Telephone: 215-884-7676 Website: www.ccef.org/

PART ONE:

GOD DETERMINES THE AGENDA

The first point of a Biblical Covenant introduces God as the transcendent One -- the Sovereign who initiates and dictates the terms of the covenant.

In this first section you will find that God has a prior claim on your child. As a covenant child, your youngster belongs to God. He has given your little one to you on loan, and He holds you responsible. He never wants you to forget that He is in charge. You'll find all this in chapter one: **Where Do Babies Come From?**

Where Do Babies Come From?

The Covenantal Facts of Life

1. Forget the Stork

I have four daughters, so I know about what happens between a man and a woman who are married (or ought to be). And I know about sperm and ova, about gestation periods and birth. But all that is actually about **how babies get here**, not **where they come from**. Actually, instead of **where**, I should ask, *"From whom do babies come?"* I can hear someone say, "Oh, I know what you're getting at... a baby comes from its mother." But Eve, the first mother, saw it quite differently.

> And Adam knew Eve his wife; and she conceived and bare Cain, and said, I have gotten a man *from the LORD* (Genesis 4:1, emphasis added).

The first mother said that her baby came from the Lord.

We can find this truth elaborated in Psalm 139:13, which says,

> Thou has covered me in my mother's womb. I will praise Thee, for I am fearfully and wonderfully made: marvelous are Thy works; and that my soul knoweth right well.

John Calvin's *Commentary on the Book of Psalms* unfolds the meaning for us:

> The "covering" here spoken of, is illustrated by Job x.2, where God is said to have "clothed us with skin and fenced us with bones and sinews." "A work so astonishing," observes Bishop Horne, "that before the Psalmist proceeds in his description of it, he cannot help breaking forth in rapture at the thought: 'I will praise thee, for I am fearfully and wonderfully made.'"[2]

---

[2] *Calvin's Commentaries,* Baker Books, Grand Rapids, 2003 (reprint), Vol. VI, James Anderson, tr. p. 213, fn.

What the Psalmist is telling us, then, is that God put him together in the womb. Another commentator[3] says that *covered* carries with it the idea of weaving or plaiting -- a graphic picture of the creator fashioning a new person in the womb. The next time you look at your little lass or laddie, remember that from the raw material of DNA, proteins and other nutrients, God formed your baby. Just as personally and individually as He made Adam from the dust of the earth, so the Lord God wove your child in the womb.

The raw materials are a little different from those that He utilized to make Adam, but the Creator is the same. You, the parent, served as the storehouse for those hereditary raw materials. That's why we say that Billy has Dad's nose, and Jenny has Mom's eyes. But since it was God who took those resources and turned them into a person, we can also say that just as surely as Adam owed his life and being to God, so does your baby.

That means that God has a prior claim on your little child, just as He does on you and your forbears all the way back to Adam and Eve. God made each of us, and we must not forget that when it comes to the agenda for our children. We all have our ideas on who our children are, how we will train them up and what we hope them to become. Dreams and aspirations are not necessarily sinful, but they must give way to the reality that God's agenda takes priority over our own.

In a very real sense, you hold your children in trust. As God's trustee, you must adopt His goals, program and methods for bringing up the child He has given over to

---

[3]Keil and Delitzsch, *Old Testament Commentaries,* Associated Publishers and Authors, Grand Rapids, (reprint, n.d.), Vol. IV, p.309.

your care. If you are a true Christian, this will not be as burdensome as it might sound, for the Holy Spirit has put in your heart an affinity for those things which please Him. You will need to consider your child-rearing carefully, however, for God has given you a trust of great value.

You can find a passage that speaks of children as a valued trust in Psalm 127:3.

> *Lo, children are an heritage of the LORD: and the*
> *fruit of the womb is His reward.*

This passage likens children to a valuable endowment that we receive from a wealthy benefactor. Your child is precious to God, and he should be precious to you as well. Contrary to the attitude of secular humanist society, **children are a blessing from God** rather than a burden.

2. Different...Yet Same

In the film *The Karate Kid*, there is a scene where the swarthy Daniel shows a picture of himself with his blond, blue-eyed girl friend to his mentor, Mr. Miyagi. Miyagi studies the two in the photo. Then he comments, "Different...yet same." From my own experience, this terse observation applies in ways far beyond what the old Okinawan gentleman intended.

When our older daughters were still in the early grades, people with problem children would comment to us, "Just wait until they become teenagers -- then you'll see." Misery loves company, and so they wished upon my wife and me the same kind of teens they had produced. Then when my girls entered into their teens without the slightest resemblance to witches, were-wolves or vampires, the comments changed to, "Well, you have girls, but boys are more headstrong."

These parents did not understand the full import of the truth: different...yet same. Yes, preteens and teens are different, but a child allowed to rebel in his early days will go on to rebel with the same spirit in adolescence. Boys and girls obviously differ, but God in His Word does not give us different programs for training them. Girls can be headstrong, too.

One of our daughters[4] was as willful as any boy I've ever observed. She would pick the most trivial issues on which to challenge us -- *e.g.,* "Let's put your shoes on so you can go outside and play." She'd look me straight in the eye as she set her jaw and planted her feet, and I knew we were in for a contest of wills. The fact that she actually **wanted** to go outside, took a back seat to the contest. She defied her mother and me on a nearly daily basis all through toddlerhood.

Another daughter was a negotiator. Almost anything we might tell her to do brought a counterproposal. This form of disobedience was much more subtle, for before I realized it, I often found myself entering into the negotiation process on her terms. She was different from her sister...yet the same.

My point is that all children share certain things in common. They are all, for example, human beings created in the image of God. They also inherited a sin-nature from conception (Psalm 51:5). Covenant children (children of Christian parents) also share certain things in common. (I will cover those promises and blessings in the next chapter.)

The common nature shared by all children points to their common origin. As the ultimate originator, God knows that the same issues arise in the lives of all

---

[4]I shall not embarrass her by giving her name.

children. Therefore His Word teaches us that as sinners they all need to learn obedience; but as people made in His image, they all need love, support and encouragement. The fact that we can determine conditions common to all children should come as a relief and a comfort to you.

As a parent, you can enjoy the uniqueness of each child without despairing over how to handle the core issues. You can recognize each individual and encourage each one's characteristic interests and aptitudes, while at the same time you understand and apply God's own standards and goals to all your children. Let me tell you why this is so important.

I once served as the principal of a Christian Day School operated by a local church. During recess one day, I observed the pastor's son and his schoolmates playing baseball. Every few minutes an argument broke out over whether someone had touched a base, ticked the ball with the bat, or some other point that affected which way the game was going. The boys yelled, used intemperate language with that in-your-face posture they picked up from watching their heroes on TV, and they would throw the bat, their gloves and the ball. It was obvious that if this continued, someone would get hurt.

Since his son was involved, I mentioned the angry outbursts to the pastor with the intention of coming to an agreement about how to stop this behavior. I was shocked to find out that he did not want to curb his son's temper; he wanted to encourage it. He said that he did not want his son to grow up to be a wimp, and that arguing and even fighting would cause him to grow up to be a *real* man. I understood that he was indirectly telling me that I was not a real man because I saw a problem with his son's anger.

As a man of the Book, he should have known better. He should have known that human wrath does not produce godliness (James 1:20). The Bible does say that sometimes it's necessary for a man to fight -- but not over the childish desire to come out ahead in some game. That pastor had substituted his own [wimpy!] juvenile idea of what makes a real man for the standard set down in the Bible. You must take care to learn from his mistake and accept God's authority in all you think and do as a parent.

The rest of this book grows out of the major theme of this chapter: that your children come from God, and that He alone has the authority and the knowledge to determine how you can and should rear your children. If you follow His direction, I cannot guarantee that your life as a parent will be free of care, distress, or even heartbreak. I can tell you that the fruits of rearing your children in the covenant will far outweigh any cost you incur. For only as you follow the guidance found in His Word will you be able to fully enjoy your children as blessings and treasures from God.

PART TWO:

GOD APPOINTS PARENTS

AS HIS AGENTS

The second point of the covenant addresses hierarchy or the chain of command. God appoints his representatives and holds them responsible for fulfilling their obligations.

In this second section you will read about fathers (and mothers) as God's agents to bring up children. As you read **Life in the Covenant with Father**, you will find out what marvelous promises God has made regarding covenant children and the conditions he lays down for the fulfillment of those promises

In **Reap Huge Profits** you will learn that Christian parents have the opportunity to collect eternal dividends from the business of rearing godly children.

Life in the Covenant with Father:

How to Understand the Biblical Principle of Covenant Succession

Faithful parenting will result, by covenanted grace, in believing children. -- Robert S. Rayburn

1. See How Abraham Represents the Model Covenant Father

And, ye fathers, provoke not your children to wrath, but bring them up in the nurture and admonition of the Lord. Ephesians 6:3

This familiar scripture zeroes in on a truth indispensable to the subject of rearing New Covenant children: the vital responsibility of covenant fathers. You'll find this emphasis in the Old Testament, as well:

> *And these words which I command thee this day, shall be in thine heart. And thou shalt teach them diligently unto thy children, and shalt talk of them when thou sittest in thine house, and when thou walkest by the way, and when thou liest down, and when thou risest up....(Deuteronomy 6:6-7).*

Scripture directs the community of faith as well, but in a more negative way (*i.e.,* do not cause them to stumble, *Matthew 18:6 et. al.*). Clearly, God lays the primary burden for training children in faith and godliness squarely on parents, particularly the fathers. This truth comes into bold relief as you investigate and come to understand the seed-truths -- both spoken and implied -- in God's covenant with Abraham.

Abram, whose name means *exalted father*, received a call and a promise from God which we see formalized into a covenant in Genesis 15. The promise included a multitude of descendants extending to many nations Abraham the *patriarch* (Hebrews 7:4) is the model and

24

prototype for covenant *father*hood.[5] Romans 4:11 describes him as the father of all who believe. The Jews called him father (John 8: 53). Even the rich man in hell lifted up his eyes and called, "Father Abraham" (Luke 16: 23). Abraham, moreover, serves as the benchmark by which you can measure both your potential and your responsibility as a father.

God's assurance that He would fulfill His covenant promise lay behind the change of Abram's name to Abraham (father of a multitude). This emphasis on fatherhood was present in the very name of the one with whom God made the Covenant of Promise. Indeed, the promise -- and the covenant itself -- turned upon the necessity that an aged, childless Abram father a son. A failure for Abraham to live up to his name as father would render fulfillment of the covenant impossible.

You see the concept of fatherhood in the warp and woof of the Abrahamic covenant. He who was father in name became father indeed, as Yahweh fulfilled His covenant promise. In the context of this very promise Abram *"believed in the LORD; and He counted it to him for righteousness"* (Genesis 15: 6).

Indeed, the future fulness of justification (counting as righteous all who believe on Christ) hung, humanly speaking, upon Abraham. For the Seed -- that distant Descendant, -- was to come from Abraham's loins. You would be hard-pressed to find a human exemplar of covenant fatherhood with a role more crucial than the one filled by Father Abraham. Therefore I'd like you to take a closer look into the covenantal role to which God appointed him, in order to more fully understand and fulfill our own responsibilities as covenant fathers.

---

[5] patri- = father; -arch = first (in rank or importance).

2. Notice What Conditions God May or May not Have Placed on Abraham

Some discussion (mainly in premilllennial, dispensational circles) has arisen over the issue of whether the promises in Yahweh's covenant with Abraham are conditioned upon Abraham's faith and obedience or not. Charles Ryrie, for example, has written,

> The ratification ceremony described in Genesis 15:9-17 when compared with near Eastern custom indicates that God alone obligated Himself to fulfill the terms of the covenant since only He walked between the pieces of the sacrificial animals. The significance of that is striking: It means that God swore fidelity to His promises and placed the obligation on [sic] their fulfillment on Himself alone. Abraham made no such oath; he was in a deep sleep, yet aware of what God promised....Clearly the Abrahamic Covenant was not conditioned on anything Abraham would or would not do; its fulfillment in all its parts depends only on God's doings.[6]

In the ancient Hebrew world, when men made a covenant, they were said to *cut a covenant*. This terminology came from the method they used to ratify it. The parties would cut a sacrificial animal in two, and then they would both pass between the pieces. By this symbolic act they swore that the one who broke the covenant should also be cut in two.

Ryrie's view has the merit of accounting for the way in which God ratified the covenant by representatively passing between the sacrificial altars in the form of a smoking oven and a flaming torch while Abraham remained passive. This raises a problem, however, with a related text.

---

[6]*Basic Theology*, Scripture Press, Wheaton, IL, 1986, pp.454-455

In the eighteenth chapter of Genesis we read of God's intention to rain judgment on Sodom. At that time the Lord said,

> Shall I hide from Abraham that thing which I do; seeing that Abraham shall surely become a great and mighty nation, and all the nations of the earth shall be blessed in him? For I know him, that he will command his children and his household after him, and they shall keep the way of the LORD, to do justice and judgment; **that the LORD may bring upon Abraham that which he hath spoken of him** (vv.17-19, emphasis added).

Notice that Abraham's successful command (or instruction[7]) of his offspring constitutes the *condition* (*i.e., "...*that the LORD may bring upon Abraham....") on which the covenant blessings depend. This passage thus leads us to conclude that the Abrahamic Covenant is conditional, contrary to the evidence of Genesis 15. The two positions, however, are not hard to reconcile.

If you want to reconcile the two views, you need to remember that some aspects of God's covenant are unconditional (*e.g.,* the coming of Christ, the promised seed), while others require an obedient faith. Consider the words of Floyd Barackman:

> This covenant is gracious. While the fulfillment of the promises relating to the patriarchs' personal lives was conditioned upon their obedience to God, those promises relating to Christ appear to be unconditional.[8]

This interpretation harmonizes well with the teaching of

---

[7]"Command is used for the instruction of a father to a son (I Sam 17: 20).... It reflects a firmly structured society in which people were responsible to their right to rule by God's command.... R. Laird Harris, ed., *Theological Wordbook of the Old Testament*, Moody Press, Chicago, 1980, Vol.2, p. 757.

[8]*Practical Christian Theology*, Practical Press, Bible School Park, NY, 1981, p. 89.

some theologians that the **Covenant of Grace** (God's covenant with the elect) and the **Covenant of Redemption** (the Father's covenant with the Son) are two aspects of one single covenant. When we apply this systematic insight to the text in Genesis, we can conclude that from the individual's point of view, the blessings of the covenant come only in fulfillment of conditions, while from the point of view of God's eternal plan, He will unconditionally bring His purposes to pass.[9]

3. Recognize the Condition God's Covenant Placed on Abraham

In Genesis twenty-two we read the account of Abraham's testing by Yahweh. Abraham passed the test by his willingness to sacrifice the son of promise. God then repeated His promise to Abraham:

> That in blessing I will bless thee, and in multiplying I will multiply thy seed as the stars of the heaven, and as the sand which is upon the sea shore: and thy seed shall possess the gate of his enemies: and in thy seed shall all the nations of the earth be blessed; **because thou hast obeyed My voice** (vv. 17-18, emphasis added).

God could not make it any plainer that the promised blessing (Hebrews 6:13-17) came in answer to Abraham's fulfillment of the condition of obedience. He obeyed to the point of putting his son on the altar and laying hold of the sacrificial knife.

At this juncture our father Abraham had given up his own agenda regarding his son and his seed's destiny. At an earlier time he had tried to pursue an agenda with regard to his wife's maid, Hagar, and her son,

---

[9]See L. Berkhof, *Systematic Theology,* Eerdman's, Grand Rapids, 1963 (1939, 1941), pp. 262-270.

Ishmael. Now, however, he was content to let God determine Isaac's life (Hebrews 11:17-19) and inheritance in the covenant. He had found that the key to covenant blessing lay in following God's agenda rather than keeping his own secret agenda in reserve. Abraham had become the model for covenant fatherhood.

God instituted the responsibilities of covenant fatherhood as a condition for covenant blessing. He stipulated that Abraham *command his children and his household after him, and they shall keep the way of the LORD, to do justice and judgment....* Thus the covenant father receives from God the authority and responsibility to train his children in the ways of the covenant Lord. Bring him up in the way God prescribes, and the child inherits the blessings of the covenant seed. This is another way of saying that the agenda for the covenant child comes from God, not the parent.

Notice, moreover, that God's condition also contains an implicit promise. *[H]e will command his children and his household after him, and they shall keep the way of the LORD.* This verse strongly implies that when the covenant father command-instructs his covenant offspring, the children will become covenant keepers rather than covenant breakers.

Now let's isolate the elements of promise and condition given by God to Abraham as follows:

1) Covenant-keepers inherit the covenant blessings;[10]

2) Covenant children become covenant-keepers

---

[10] I have referred to this concept by the term *covenant succession.*

when faithfully command-instructed by the covenant fathers;

3) Therefore the fulfillment of God's promise of covenant succession is conditioned upon faithful command/instruction on the part of covenant fathers.

Although this line of thought may seem quite foreign to preaching and practice today, former generations have recognized and promoted it.

The Puritan commentator Matthew Henry had this to say about Abraham's responsibilities as a covenant father:

...God having made the covenant with him and with his seed, and his household being circumcised pursuant to that, he was very careful to teach and rule them well. Those that expect family blessings must make conscience of family duty. If our children be the Lord's, they must be nursed for him; if they wear his livery, they must be trained up in his work....Abraham, herein, had an eye to posterity, and was in care not only that his household with him, but that his household after him, should keep the way of the Lord.... **His doing this was the fulfilling of the conditions of the promises which God had made to him.**[11]

With this observation Matthew Henry affirms the doctrine that those covenant parents who faithfully command-instruct their children will see them grow up into covenant keepers who practice their parents' faith and inherit all the blessings of the covenant (salvation included). This is what covenant succession means.

---

[11] *Commentary on the Whole Bible*, MacDonald Publishing, McLean VA, n.d., Vol. I, p.118, emphasis added.

4. Witness that Covenant Succession Appears in the Rest of the Old Testament

God constructed the skeletal framework of covenant succession in His covenant with Abraham. What really interests and affects you and me, though, is whether Father Abraham was unique in this regard, or if today we also can claim the promise of covenant succession. That is, *if you properly command/instruct your children, will they grow up faithful to Christ?* If you and I can find the promise of covenant succession in the rest of Scripture and see that God meant it for all His children, we will know that the promise applies to your children and mine.

Now let us consider just a few of the passages that deal with covenant offspring. We can begin by looking at Psalm 37: 9-11 & 24-26.

> *For evildoers shall be cut off: but those that wait upon the LORD, they shall inherit the earth. For yet a little while, and the wicked shall not be: yea, thou shalt diligently consider his place, and it shall not be. But the meek shall inherit the earth; and shall delight themselves in the abundance of peace* (vv.9-11).

Plainly, the passage teaches us that, ultimately, covenant breakers lose by coming under God's judgment, and covenant keepers win by inheriting God's blessing.

The Psalmist includes the covenant keeper's seed in the covenant blessing as follows:

> *Though he fall, he shall not be utterly cast down: for the LORD upholdeth him with his hand. I have been young, and now am old; yet have I not seen the righteous forsaken, **nor his seed begging bread.** He is ever merciful, and lendeth; **and his seed is blessed*** (vv. 24-26, emphasis added).

Here we find that the Lord's blessing falls not only upon the covenant keeper, but upon his children as well.

The above-cited passage is not an isolated instance. Consider these verses:

> Praise ye the LORD. Blessed is the man that feareth the LORD, that delighteth greatly in his commandments. **His seed shall be mighty upon earth:** the generation of the upright shall be blessed (Psalm 112:1-2, emphasis added.)

Again we see that Scripture includes the children when it speaks of blessings on those who keep covenant with God. Furthermore,

> What man is he that fears the LORD? Him shall he teach in the way that he shall choose. His soul shall dwell at ease; **and his seed shall inherit the earth.** The secret of the LORD is with them that fear him; and he will shew them his covenant (Psalm 25: 12-14).

Since (1) only the righteous inherit (Psalm 37:29), when the psalmist says (2) that the seed of the covenant keeper will also inherit, he reveals an underlying assumption -- that the offspring of the covenant people will grow up to embrace -- and to persevere in -- the covenant faith of their parents, and that they will inherit the earth.

We shall conclude our brief look at covenant succession in the Psalter with an even more explicit promise as found in Psalm 102:28:

> The children of Thy servants shall continue, and their seed shall be established before Thee.

We can hardly find a more definite declaration of God's intention that His covenant promises should follow generational lines.

In the Book of Proverbs we find practical wisdom in applying God's commandments to our everyday lives. It should not surprise us, then, that we find here many references to child-rearing. At this point let's look at just two that pertain to the **conditions** of covenant suc-

32

cession. The first is familiar. It says,

> Train up a child in the way he should go: and
> when he is old he will not depart from it. (Proverbs
> 22:6)

Here we see that the father's[12] faithfulness in training up his child fulfills the condition of God's covenant promise and assures that the child will persevere in the faith. God here uses the language of cause and effect Do this, and here is the result that will follow.

The second verse uses even more forceful language to drive home the point that a father's discipline fulfills a critical condition in guaranteeing the child's salvation. Proverbs 23:13-14 tells us,

> Withhold not correction from the child: for if thou
> beatest him with the rod, he shall not die. Thou
> shalt beat him with the rod, and shalt deliver his
> soul from hell.

According to this passage, God considers it instrumental to the child's salvation that the father spank him within the context of Biblical **correction**,[13]

Some people object that if parental discipline saved souls, then it would take salvation out of God's hands and place it in the hands of man. "Salvation would no longer lie in individuals coming to God by faith in Christ," they say, "but in the acts of their parents."

To this I reply that a child properly reared is saved by faith alone, in Christ alone. Parental discipline is not the means of the child's salvation. It is rather the satisfaction of a requirement which God has freely chosen as the condition on which He will fulfill His promise. The

---

[12] Solomon wrote Proverbs (under Divine inspiration) to his son.

[13] We will cover the proper use of the rod in chapters six & seven, so do not think that indiscriminate or unwise beating fulfills this covenant condition. You must follow Scriptural procedures with godly motives.

Holy Spirit will work in the child's heart in fulfillment of the covenant promise to work saving faith in the child's heart (Ephesians 2:8-9).

This may be easier to understand if you consider how God uses life circumstances to bring some to Christ. Often an individual will slide into sin and hit bottom. Then, when he is down and out, the Holy Spirit uses the misery caused by his sin to turn him to Christ. In the same way the Holy Spirit works in, with and through fatherly discipline to bring a child to Christ.

For the Calvinists among my readers, I will restate the issue by saying that the same God who predestines the results also predestines the fulfillment of the conditions. I'm sure you don't believe that the promise to save all who believe limits God's freedom. On the contrary, you see that He who made the condition freely guarantees its fulfillment among His elect. Likewise, God has conditioned the surety of the covenant child's salvation on proper discipline by the parent. Therefore, God Himself determines its fulfillment among His elect.

The final Old Testament passage I want to present appears in Malachi. In the passage the prophet is making a point about the purpose of marriage. He proceeds to tell the unfaithful and divorce-prone husband why God instituted the marriage covenant. Speaking of the wife, he says she is

> ...thy companion, and the wife of thy covenant.
> And did not He make one?.... And wherefore one?
> That He might seek a godly seed (2:14-15).

Here we find that God's purpose for the covenant of marriage is that godly offspring might be raised up. This stated purpose dovetails perfectly with all the other Scriptures that speak about covenant succession. It demonstrates the Lord's rationale for making such a promise in the first place: to raise up a godly seed (offspring), culminating in the appearance of **the Seed** of the woman, our Lord Jesus Christ. This brings us to the question of whether or not the promise of covenant succession continues on into the New Testament.

5. Understand that Covenant Succession Applies to New Testament Believers

> *Then there were brought unto Him little children, that He should put His hands on them, and pray: and the disciples rebuked them. But Jesus said, Suffer little children, and forbid them not, to come unto Me: for of such is the Kingdom of Heaven. And He laid His hands on them, and departed thence* (Matthew 19:13-15).

Since only those who believed in Jesus would have brought their children for His blessing, you can be sure that the children mentioned here come from covenant households. Therefore we can draw at least one definite conclusion about covenant succession from this passage.[14] Jesus proclaims that the Kingdom of Heaven is comprised of such as these infant children of the covenant. He declares that these privileged little ones define His kingdom (even though many adults say that little children cannot believe on Him).

The Greek word *child* is *pais*, a general term that includes all minor children. The word used in the passage above is the diminutive form, *paidion,* which strictly denotes a little child and applies to the whole range of ages from newborn through (at least) toddlerhood. Thus, when Jesus uses the word, He is referring to all children in that age bracket including infants.

---

[14]Since our Lord said to *suffer* (allow, permit) the little children to come to Him, we might also conclude that children of obedient Christian parents will have a certain affinity, an *effectual call* from the Holy Spirit that draws them to the Savior.

In the eighteenth chapter of Matthew's Gospel we find an extended passage that likewise speaks to the doctrine of covenant succession. Did you know that Jesus' teachings about cutting off the offending hand or plucking out the offending eye as well as His parable about the ninety and nine all occur in the context of His teaching about the importance of **little** covenant children? You needn't take my word for it -- read verses one through fourteen and see for yourself.

At the same time came the disciples unto Jesus, saying, Who is the greatest in the kingdom of heaven? And Jesus called a little child unto Him, and set him in the midst of them, and said, Verily I say unto you, except ye be converted, and become as little children, ye shall not enter into the kingdom of heaven. Whosoever therefore shall humble himself as this little child, the same is greatest in the kingdom of heaven. And whoso shall receive one such little child in My name receiveth Me.

But whoso shall offend one of these little ones which believe in Me, it were better for him that a millstone were hanged about his neck, and that he were drowned in the depth of the sea.

Woe unto the world because of offences! for it must needs be that offences come; but woe to that man by whom the offence cometh! Wherefore if thy hand or thy foot offend thee, cut them off, and cast them from thee: it is better for thee to enter into life halt or maimed, rather than having two hands or two feet to be cast into everlasting fire. And if thine eye offend thee, pluck it out, and cast it from thee: it is better for thee to enter into life with one eye, rather than having two eyes to be cast into hell fire.

Take heed that ye despise not one of these little ones; for I say unto you, That in heaven their angels do always behold the face of my Father which is in heaven. For the Son of man is come to save that which was lost. How think ye? if a man have an hundred sheep, and one of them be gone astray, doth he not leave the ninety and nine, and goeth into the mountains, and seeketh that which is gone astray? And if so be that he find it, verily I say unto you, he rejoiceth more of that sheep, than of the ninety and nine which went not astray. Even so it is not the will of your Father which is in heaven that one of these little ones should perish.

This scripture covers a lot of ground, so I will point out once again that the passage has a recurring major theme -- covenant children. Now let's look over some highlights from this passage.

Notice that in addressing the adults in His audience, Jesus tells them that conversion equates to becoming like one of the little covenant children in their midst.[15] We can see from this passage how our Lord teaches that even very young children[16] from covenant households have a place in the kingdom.

Adults outside the New Covenant need to undergo conversion in order to enter the Kingdom of God. Jesus, however ascribes kingdom status to children of the covenant. He places the covenant child on the same level as an adult who has repented and believed on Him. He also continues by referring to covenant children then present as *these little ones which believe in Me.*

Furthermore, our Lord says that to receive a covenant child amounts to the same thing as receiving Him. The

---

[15] Jesus refers to these little ones as those who believe on Him. He also makes the point that the children He refers to have angels who are before the Father's face. Therefore, He is not speaking of pagan children or children in general as some teach.

[16] The word *paidion* is used throughout the passage, so infants are included in this age grouping.

Priest King identifies with these little ones, and this speaks of covenant representation. Therefore He is Mediator and Advocate not only for adult believers but for the youngest children of the covenant as well. Thus when the Divine Advocate of believers' children threatens dire consequences for causing one of them to stumble[17] (i.e., ensnare them into or cause them to fall into sin or unbelief), you and I had best pay close heed. When He goes on to say that we must exercise caution not to make ourselves stumble, some commentators say that is because we, too, are His little ones, but I think there is a better explanation.

Why would a caution against causing ourselves to stumble appear in the middle of a warning against tripping up little ones? I believe it is because so often our own entanglement in sin leads to ensnaring others, particularly our own children. The father who repeatedly indulges his anger or lust teaches his children by example. What's more, he has created an atmosphere which excuses and gives tacit approval to the child's own sin. Thus it is far better to lose a hand or an eye than to entangle ourselves in sins which may also ensnare our children and will certainly bring us into the kind of woe about which our Savior warns.

Finally, we see the value that Jesus (and the Father) place on children born into the covenant. He says that we must not despise them or hold them in low regard.[18] The parable of the ninety-nine underscores the trouble which the Shepherd will take in order to save just one covenant child. Jesus gives the parable's

---

[17]The verb *skandalizo*, translated "offend" means **to set a snare for** or **to put a stumblingblock in front of.**

[18]Many people think that the word **despise** is interchangeable with the word **hate**, which is incorrect. It means to disdain or hold in low esteem.

interpretation in the last sentence of the passage. *Even so it is not the will of your Father which is in heaven, that **one of these little ones** should perish.*

From this passage we can extract certain generalities about Jesus' teaching concerning covenant succession:

> 1) We must ascribe covenant status to covenant children;
>
> 2) A covenant child may stumble and not persevere in the faith;[19]
>
> 3) Whoever ensnares the covenant child is held accountable for causing him to stumble
>
> 4) God's purpose and pleasure concerning the covenant is that covenant children be saved.

You find in this passage concepts that mirror those we found in God's comments regarding Abraham and covenant succession (Genesis 19:17-19, see above). Therefore Christian fathers also bear a weighty responsibility to command-instruct their children to keep covenant with God.

Before we move on to the next New Testament passage, I want you to try to put yourself into the same covenant mindset as a first century Israelite who has heard Jesus teach. You know about God's promise to Abraham concerning the succession of his offspring to the covenant promise, and you have familiarity with the Psalms that speak about covenant succession. Now you are in Jerusalem on the day of Pentecost, listening

---

[19]We are not here talking about loss of salvation, but about the fact that some children will fall away and not be saved. From God's standpoint, these children are not among the elect. From ours, both the unbelieving child and the one who causes him to stumble bear responsibility.

to Peter's sermon. He comes to a crucial point:

> Repent and be baptized every one of you in the name of Jesus Christ for the remission of sins, and ye shall receive the gift of the Holy Ghost. For the promise is unto **you, and to your children,** and to all that are afar off, even as many as the Lord our God shall call (Acts 2:38-39, emphasis added).

Now, as a first-century parent with an understanding of the scriptures we presented above, would you not hear these words and conclude that the gospel message preached by Peter included your children's inheritance of the covenant promises?

The Apostle Paul confirms this point in his letter to the church at Corinth. At one point he addresses believers with unbelieving spouses:[20]

> And the woman which hath an husband that believeth not, and if he be pleased to dwell with her, let her not leave him. For the unbelieving husband is sanctified by the wife, and the unbelieving wife is sanctified by the husband: else were your children unclean; but now are they holy[21] (I Corinthians 7:13-14).

It seems that in this special instance a believer confers a certain limited covenant status on his/her unbelieving spouse.[22] This limited status does not include salvation (see verse 16)[23], but it obviously exists for the sake of

---

[20]He is not advocating marriage to an unbeliever; rather, he speaks to those who have come to Christ after marriage.

[21]The word here translated *holy* is rendered *saints* in chapter one, verse two.

[22]Marriage is, after all, a covenant (Malachi 2:14).

[23]I would surmise that since marriage itself is a covenant established to raise up godly seed (Malachi 2:14-15), it is the unbeliever's acquiescence to the covenant with his believing spouse that "sanctifies" him/her to raise up covenant children to God. In other words, he/she is not in covenant with God, but is in covenant with a spouse who is in covenant with God.

the children and their succession to the promises of the covenant (Acts 2:38-39).

6. Recognize the Conditions that Apply to New Covenant Fathers

Jesus and the apostles have made it plain that the promise of covenant succession holds true in the New Covenant. You may rest in the assurance of God's promise that your children will grow up in the faith and persevere in their faithfulness to Christ all their lives. The fulfillment of the promise, however, will only come when you satisfy the same conditions which God placed upon Abraham:

> For I know him, that he will command his children and his household after him, and they shall keep the way of the LORD, to do justice and judgment; **that the LORD may bring upon Abraham that which he hath spoken of him** (Genesis 18:19, emphasis added).

We can see from certain New Testament passages that this condition is still in effect.

We call the letters that Paul wrote to Timothy and Titus *Pastoral Epistles* because of the subject matter found in them. It should not surprise us, then, that they contain God's standards for entry into the ministry.

> A bishop[24] then must be blameless, the husband of one wife....one that ruleth well his own house, **having his children in subjection with all gravity**.... (I Timothy 3:2, 4, emhasis added).

Notice that the candidate for ministry - the father - is held accountable for his children's behavior. No exceptions, no excuses...if the children are out of control, the blame rests squarely on Dad's shoulders. Further, this is not Paul's only teaching on the subject.

---

[24] overseer or pastor

In his letter to Titus, Paul gives a similar list of pastoral standards. In this context he makes the conditionality of covenant succession even more clear:

> If any man be blameless, the husband of one wife, **having faithful children**...(Titus 1:6, emphasis added).

Here we find that the father must bear responsibility not only for his children's outward behavior, but for the inner life of their hearts as well. He must not only bring his children into subjection to his paternal rule, but he must reasonably demonstrate that he has brought them up to be **faithful** as well.

The Greek word here translated *faithful* is *pistos* which can mean *believing*, as it certainly does in Galatians 3:9: *...are blessed with **faithful** Abraham.* If Paul used *pistos* in this sense in Titus 1:6, he would have meant that the ability to bring up children who believe is a qualification for the ministry. If, on the other hand, one insists that *pistos* here simply means faithful, we must ask, "Faithful to whom or what?"

If the requirement is that his children be faithful to Christ, then we have a stronger case for the father's responsibility. He must not just bring up chidren who profess the faith. He must rear children who actually demonstrate faithfulness to the Savior. In the unlikely event that Paul means that children should demonstrate faithfulness to their father, we must point out that children truly faithful to a Christian father will also be faithful to his God and Savior.

The fact that God makes the ability to rear godly, obedient, believing children a prerequisite for entry into the ministry provides us with a strong case that such a goal is **attainable**. The promise that God will save children who are brought up correctly is not some pie-in-the-sky unrealistic ideal. God intends that men who set their sights on the ministry of the Word successfully rear their children in the faith. Furthermore, since ministers serve as teachers[25] and examples[26], they should possess the ability to show others how to do the same. When you stop and think about it, this makes great sense.

One of the main duties of a pastor involves discipling the people of his congregation, both childen and adults. Why should anyone think it odd to require a candidate to submit a **living resume** as embodied in his children to see how good he is at actually making disciples? After all, the Word does make the point that, *[I]f a man know not how to rule his own house, how shall he take care of the church of God?*

The lives and character of his children reveal much about the ministerial candidate's understanding of Scripture as well as his understanding of how to apply the Scriptures to the problems of others in a real-life context. This reveals more than how well he may perform in the pulpit; it reveals how he will function as shepherd, leader, counselor and friend to the people under his charge. On top of that, it will probably tell you what kind of help to expect from him in training up your own children.

I hope you see that the Bible not only teaches your obligation to train up Christian children, but it also reveals that you, Christian mother, and especially you, Christian father, will be able, by God's grace, to raise up your children as heirs of the promise and faithful followers of Christ. To confirm you in your resolve, you might want to acquaint yourself with objections to the

---

[25]I Timothy 3:2; II Timothy 2:24.
[26]I Peter 5:3.

doctrine and Biblical answers to those objections.

6. Find Answers to Objections

Objection: I am a Calvinist, and if what you say were true, it would limit the freedom of God in election. Man would have the power to determine who is saved and lost.

Answer: The promise of covenant succession does not limit God's freedom any more than the invitation, *Whosoever will, let him take the water of life freely* (Revelation 22:17). The same God who made both promises has decreed from eternity who will fulfill the conditions of the promises and who will not.

Objection: Your doctrine breaks down with the Scriptural examples of Ishmael and Esau. They both could have inherited the covenant promise, but God chose that they would not (see Genesis 21:9-12, Malachi 1:2-3, Romans 9:6-13).

Answer: Remember that the covenant promise of succession depended for its fulfillment on how the covenant father command-instructed his children (Genesis 18:19). Scripture is silent about how much input Abraham had in rearing Ishamael or its quality. Hagar may or may not have borne the lion's share of responsibility in bringing up Ishmael. The point is, Scripture does not tell us. Likewise in Esau's case, the Bible does not say how Isaac reared him. It does hint, however, that since Esau was Isaac's favorite, his father may have had the stronger influence in his upbringing. Rebekah, then, may have had more influence on Jacob. Believing parents do not always raise each of their children the same way. Since the Bible does not give us specifics on the kind of parenting that Ishmael and Esau received, we must

44

focus on what it **does** say. It says that children properly command-instructed by their parents will grow up faithful to the Lord.

Objection: I believe that you have taken general statements of Scripture and ascribed qualities to them that God never intended. I believe the passages you cite supply us with a generality that covenant children will usually grow up to continue in the faith, but not all of them. We should look on this as the usual course of events, but not as a hard and fast rule.

Answer: We have no other way to determine what God intends in Scripture than by what He says. When He tells us, *Train up a child in the way he should go, and when he is old he will not depart from it,* how shall we understand Him? and when He tells a father that disciplining a son will *save his soul from hell,* how shall we interpret His words?

I take these plain statements of God's Word quite literally. I do not see any place where God has qualified His statements on covenant succession. Therefore, I have a question for you who wish to see these statements as something other than literal promises. For a moment let us hypothetically suppose that God **now** wanted to turn these generalities into specific promises...how could He make them any plainer?

Objection: I will concede that God promises to save the children of those who will properly bring them up. *BUT,* since we are all sinful, imperfect people, every one of us fails in some way as a parent. Therefore, it would amount to arrogance to try to claim this promise. Also, your teaching of covenant succession will tend to foster pride in the hearts of parents with believing children. They will claim credit for their children's faithfulness.

Answer: Let me answer the second part of the objection first. By the logic presented here you shouldn't witness for the Lord, because if the person comes to Christ, you will be able to take credit for it. Yes, there is the possibility of taking pride in your obedience to the Lord, just as there is the possibility of pride among those who disobey Him. The possibility of pride is not a Scriptural argument for or against any doctrine. As to the idea that the promise is void because we cannot fulfill the condition to absolute perfection, I say, let's look at the Scriptures. God said of Abraham (Genesis 18:19, cited above) that He would fulfill His covenant promise to Abraham because He knew that Abraham would successfully instruct his children after him to follow the Lord. Abraham was not sinlessly perfect.

Further, we have seen that a requirement for pastoral candidates is that they produce faithful children. Pastors also suffer from the imperfections of sin. If Abraham could do it, and pastors can do it, then you and I can also rear believing children. The standard is not one of absolute perfection, but one of consistent faithfulness (I Corinthians 4:2).

Objection: My pastor is a dedicated Christian and a wonderful Bible teacher -- but his son has rebelled against him and shows no sign of faith in Christ. I can't believe that such a good man should be held accountable for what his son does. If someone accused him of being a bad father, it would break his heart.

Answer: I believe this objection is a major reason that we do not hear the promises of covenant succession preached in our churches today. Too many fear offending this dear brother or that good sister. They fear men more than they fear God. David was a great king and a godly man. BUT as a father to Amnon, he

46

failed.[27] So Christian parents --even men of God --can fail in how they fulfill their parenting obligations. They shall suffer loss before Christ's judgment seat though they be saved as by fire (I Corinthians 3:13-15).

This truth deeply affects me as I look around at parents I have known who will suffer that kind of loss. In the meantime, let's lift up these sorrowing parents and especially their prodigal children in prayer. Perhaps God will graciously move to bring them to repentance and faith. Nevertheless, a state of denial will not change the facts concerning what the Bible teaches about covenant succession.

Conclusion

The Old and New Testaments agree in their teaching about covenant succession. We may summarize their teaching in the following points.

1. We enter into the covenant of salvation by faith.

2. To the faithful, as to Abraham, God promises to include their children in the covenant.

3. God places a condition on covenant parents (fathers in particular) that He will save their children if they train up their children properly (i.e., to be faithful to the covenant).

4. God makes it plain that child-rearing practices

---

[27] Regarding David's failure as a parent: before Amnon raped his sister Tamar, she made a telling appeal. She told him to ask David to give her to him, for he would not withhold her from Amnon. This, along with David's lack of action after the rape, strongly suggests laxity of discipline, even indulgence on his part toward Amnon.

which achieve this goal are within the reach of ordinary Christians.

Note: For further study on the doctrine of covenant succession I recommend that you read "THE PRESBYTERIAN DOCTRINES OF COVENANT CHILDREN, COVENANT NURTURE AND COVENANT SUCCESSION" by Robert S. Rayburn. The article can be found at http://www.federationorc.org/article.php?sid=4

Reap Huge Profits

For Christ and His Kingdom by Investing Your Children

1. Consider Your Balance Sheet

In my mind's eye I can look back some thirty years to our little two-room apartment. It was the home to which we brought our firstborn from the hospital. We put the bassinet in the living room, because in the middle of it was an old oil stove -- our only source of heat.

I remember looking down at my little girl, lying there totally dependent on her mother and me. I was struck with awe (and terror!) at the responsibility that seemed so suddenly thrust upon me. I realized that my child would one day, God willing, grow up to live as an adult in the world that God created.

I further realized that everybody walking around out there in creation is either an **asset** or a **liability** to God's stated program and purpose. My reflection soon turned to earnest prayer that the little baby before me would grow up to become an asset to His kingdom. My eyes mist over as I recognize how wonderfully He has answered that prayer.

I hope you have a similar vision and prayer for your own little one(s). I hope your heart is bursting with the desire that your children count as assets rather than as liabilities in God's account books. With that in mind, I would like you to read through the Scripture passage below...and think about profit and loss.

> For the kingdom of heaven is as a man traveling into a far country, who called his own servants, and delivered unto them his goods. And unto one

he gave five talents, to another two, and to another one; to every man according to his several ability; and straightway took his journey.

Then he that had received the five talents went and traded with the same, and made them other five talents. And likewise he that had received two, he also gained other two. But he that had received one went and digged in the earth, and hid his lord's money.

After a long time the lord of those servants cometh, and reckoneth with them. And so he that had received five talents came and brought other five talents, saying, Lord, thou deliveredst unto me five talents: behold, I have gained beside them five talents more. His lord said unto him, Well done, thou good and faithful servant: thou hast been faithful over a few things, I will make thee ruler over many things: enter thou into the joy of thy lord.

He also that had received two talents came and said, Lord, thou deliveredst unto me two talents: behold, I have gained two other talents beside them. His lord said unto him, Well done, good and faithful servant; thou hast been faithful over a few things, I will make thee ruler over many things: enter thou into the joy of thy lord.

Then he which had received the one talent came and said, Lord, I knew thee that thou art an hard man, reaping where thou hast not sown, and gathering where thou hast not strawed: And I was afraid, and went and hid thy talent in the earth: Lo, there thou hast that is thine. His lord answered and said unto him, Thou wicked and slothful servant, thou knewest that I reap where I sowed not, and gather where I have not strawed: Thou oughtest therefore to have put my money to the exchangers, and then at my coming I should have received mine own with usury. Take therefore the talent from him, and give it unto him which hath ten talents.

For unto every one that hath shall be given, and he shall have abundance: but from him that hath not shall be taken away even that which he hath. And cast ye the unprofitable servant into outer darkness: there shall be weeping and gnashing of teeth (Matthew 25:14-29).

2. Christ's Kingdom Has Capital Assets

Jesus said that His kingdom is like a man dividing up his goods. The goods in the parable refer to the man's **capital assets** which are considerable. He entrusts them to the people whom he considers his most reliable employees.

> **Capital Assets** are those assets which can be used to produce something. The machines in a factory are capital assets...so are a carpenter's tools. Because we can so easily convert monetary wealth by using it to purchase productive goods, we also refer to the money we invest in business as **capital.** The man in the parable had a vast sum of investment capital.

You know the story. One man received five talents and used them to go into business and turn a *profit*. He doubled his boss's investment. The man who received two talents also doubled the money his boss invested. The man who received one talent did not put it to work in a business venture. Perhaps he was afraid to risk losing the large sum for which he was accountable.

> **So...what's a talent?** The **talent** referred to in Matthew 11 is the Roman talent -- an amount of money equal to the pay for 6,000 days of labor. At six dollars an hour, figuring an eight hour day, one talent today would amount to $288,000.

51

When their wealthy patron returned, he abundantly rewarded the employees who had successfully turned a *profit*. He punished the one who did not even try. Moreover, he disclosed that the very issue which concerned him was *profitability* -- for he condemned the last servant as "*unprofitable*" (verse 30).

So, the lesson is that the Lord entrusts you with certain capital assets. He expects you to take them and to *do business*[28] in such a way as to bring profit to His kingdom. (Remember, the parable tells us what the kingdom of heaven is like.) That raises the question of what assets God has given us and for which He holds us responsible.

3. Identifying the Kingdom's Assets

God does not drop large sums of money out of the sky upon Christians for them to invest in businesses. Well, then what are the capital assets of the kingdom that He expects us to use make a profit? Theology books? ...hymnbooks?....buildings?...pews? No, the precious capital assets of Christ's kingdom do not consist in material things.

The Apostle Paul tells us that the kingdom is not defined in terms of covered dish dinners.

> *For the kingdom of God is not meat and drink; but righteousness, and peace, and joy in the Holy Ghost.* (Romans 14:17)

Christ's kingdom consists of certain spiritual qualities produced by the Holy Spirit in lives of His subjects. These qualities include righteousness (obedience to Christ as King), joy and peace (blessings of the King upon the people of His realm).

---

[28] In the parallel passage in Luke 19, the word *occupy* can be rendered "do business" (compare verses 13 and 15).

It stands to reason, then, that you can bring profit to His kingdom by delivering people into it and helping them to develop the qualities of righteousness, joy and peace that Paul mentions. This squares exactly with the Great Commission that Jesus gave to His Church. We read it in Matthew 28:18-20.

> *All power is given unto Me in heaven and in earth. Go ye, therefore, and teach all nations, baptizing them in the name of the Father, and of the Son, and of the Holy Ghost: teaching them to observe all things whatsoever I have commanded you....*

The word *teach* in *teach all nations* means to make disciples. Thus as we make disciples for our Lord, we are multiplying the assets of His kingdom. We make profit for Him by helping to introduce righteousness, peace and the joy of the Holy Spirit into the lives of others.

We should not deem it strange to speak of people as capital assets. Many top-flight businessmen have recognized their employees as their most important assets. Also, the Bible symbolically represents children as olive plants -- assets to a family's agricultural enterprise (Psalm 128:3).

But specifically and especially, what capital assets -- what life (or lives) -- has God given to you that you might disciple? Whose life (or lives) do you hold **in trust** as you hold no other? By now I'm sure you're way ahead of me, but let's look at Psalm 127:3, anyway.

> *Lo, children are an heritage of the LORD: and the fruit of the womb is His reward.*

God has entrusted you with an unspeakably precious asset: your child(ren). He expects you to enter into the business of making them profitable to His kingdom. He will hold you accountable for your efforts.[29]

Does the weight of this responsibility frighten you? If not, you haven't paid attention. I have found it scary more than once in my career as a father. The buck stops with you as a parent... *especially* if you're the dad.

Just don't let fear do to you what it did to the unprofitable servant. It paralyzed him into inaction. Don't be so afraid of doing the wrong thing that you do nothing. The unprofitable servant was not punished for trying and failing, but for not trying at all.

4. Making an Intelligent Investment

Okay, so you're willing to give it your best shot -- this business of investing your children for profit in Christ's Kingdom. Now you need to know where to start. As with any enterprise, it's good to start by figuring the cost.

> *For which of you, intending to build a tower, sitteth not down first, and counteth the cost, whether he have sufficient to finish it? Lest haply, after he hath laid the foundation, and is not able to finish it, all that behold it begin to mock him, saying, This man began to build, and was not able to finish.*
>
> *Or what king, going to make war against another king, sitteth not down first, and consulteth whether he be able with ten thousand to meet him that cometh against him with twenty thousand? Or else, while the other is yet a great way off, he sendeth an ambassage, and desireth conditions of peace.*
>
> *So likewise, whosoever he be of you that*

------

[29] I do not say that children are the **only** capital assets in Christ's kingdom, but they are the ones for which we are most directly responsible.

54

*forsaketh not all that he hath, he cannot be my
disciple* (Luke 14:28-33).

It costs everything to **be** a disciple. It costs no less to
make disciples. Everyone who ever started a business
soon found out that it demanded sacrifice. Some have
sacrificed their time, energy, leisure, and marriages for
the sake of succeeding in business. What would you
give up for the sake of succeeding in the business of
training up faithful children? Would you give up your
new car? your nice home? the job that keeps you away
from your family for long periods?

I know it's easy to excuse neglecting the family by
saying, "I'm putting in all these hours so they can have
_____ [fill in the blank]." But the business of
parenting does not revolve around providing children
with more and better and finer *things.* It turns upon
bringing up your children in the **nurture and
admonition of the Lord**. That requires time...and lots
of it.

Don't fool yourself with the idea that you can schedule
five minutes of **quality time** with your children every
evening. I can tell you from experience that those really
special quality moments can't be scheduled. They just
happen in the providence of God. And they usually
happen somewhere in the middle of the **quantity time**
you spend together.

What my grown children remember as special from
their childhood sometimes surprises me. It's usually not
the planned events, not planned by us humans,
anyway. They (and I) remember those moments that
caught us in the act of being ourselves -- in each
other's company.

One memorable, if silly, moment, occurred when I

heard Donna and Theresa evidently struggling in the next room. I found them in front of the open closet. Donna was trying to hoist her sister up high enough to reach a game on the closet shelf. I said, "Here . . . I can help you with that."

Whereupon I picked up Theresa under her arms and lifted her up to reach the game. In mid-hoist I realized how foolish it was for me to lift her up to reach something that was not even over my head. Well, it tickled my funnybone, and I began to laugh. Then both Donna and Theresa began laughing.

Before it was over I was too weak to stand. My wife, Laura, came into the room, and my weak and breathless attempts to explain what was so funny set us up for a renewed season of belly laughs. Shared experiences like this one will bond a family, but you can't schedule them. You have to make yourself available, **put in the time** and then take them as they come.

More than that, just getting to know a child takes time. I mean really knowing what makes him tick -- not just his likes and dislikes, but what motivates him, what interests him, what moves him to laughter and to tears, what strengths and weaknesses he possesses, what sins he struggles with, and what is the condition of his soul.

To do this you need to spend time watching him play and playing with him, talking to him and listening to what he says -- even if it seems unimportant to you. You need to spend time just *being* together. Lots of time being together.

When I talk about spending time in the business of parenting, I do not just mean physical presence. I've caught my own attention wandering. And when you're dog-tired, sometimes presence in body-only is the best you can do. Your family can tell whether you're really with them, though.

I know a young man in his thirties who has wanted to go into the ministry for years. He has a wife and small children, however. Study and preparation for the ministry (along with his regular full-time job), threatened to take him away from his family. He decided that to neglect his family, even for the ministry, would dishonor God.

For now, that man is concentrating his efforts on his wife and children. I respect him for making that tough decision. When his children grow up, he will be ready to enter the ministry. You see, shepherding a little flock of Christ's children is probably the best preparation for the ministry that I know.

Over the years I have seen pastors, evangelists and teachers who neglected family duties in pursuit of their ministries. I have seen some of them pay a terrible price in terms of their own children. No one ever told them that when God put them in the **child-rearing business**, it was the **most important business** of their lives.

As important as time spent with your children may be, there are other things necessary for good parenting. You will need to determine your goals and standards. You also will need to develop certain skills. We will cover these matters in other chapters.

5. A Covenantal Vision of Profit for the Kingdom

Now let's look at the nature of profit. When you invest dollars or pesos or **talents,** you normally count your profit in terms of dollars or pesos or **talents.** Remember the parable from the beginning of this chapter.

> Lord, thou deliveredst unto me five talents: behold, I have gained beside them five talents more (Matthew 25:20).

Now...since we have already determined that the assets of the Kingdom of God include children, can we conclude that the profit we reap is more children? Yes!! "And how can this be," you ask? I can answer in one word: **grandchildren**.

You rear children who grow up faithful to the Lord Jesus. They grow up and have children whom they also disciple faithfully. Now your children's children are added to your kingdom profit. And if your grandchildren follow suit, you may be in Heaven, but you'll still be collecting the returns on your initial investment.

Think of it this way -- you have three children. They grow up as profit in Christ's kingdom. They each have three children who also grow up profitably. Your own profit -- three children --plus the profit of your children -- nine children -- adds up to a profit of twelve. At the same rate, your total profit after the next generation would be thirty-nine.

A Bigger Vision: suppose you decided to have **five** children and could convince your descendants to do the same:

1st generation	=	5
2nd generation	=	25
3rd generation	=	125
4th generation	=	+625
You would be responsible for a total of		**780** Christians

If this possibility seems remote and unreal to you, consider Jonathan Edwards -- Puritan pastor of the

1700's. By 1900 his descendants numbered some 1400, including:

13 college presidents, 65 professors, two graduate school deans, 100 lawyers, 66 physicians, 80 holders of public office....[30]

We can see what an impact his posterity must have made on our nation. We have no idea, however, how successful he was in producing descendants faithful to Christ. Therefore our vision and objective must include not just producing successors -- even highly successful and respectable ones. We must seek to pass on the knowledge and skills of successful Christian parenting to future generations.

An inspection of conservative Christian churches in America will reveal just how much we need such a vision today. We find Christian parents whose children slip into lukewarmness by their early teens. By adulthood, many are lost to the world and its allure. In order to hold its own -- before it can consider growth -- each generation of the church must win unsaved adults just to make up for what it has lost among its own children.

We need to see that God means for His covenant people to grow through the normal channels of multiplication as well as through evangelistic outreach. Remember what God said about Abraham.

> For I know him, that he will command his children and his household after him, and they shall keep the way of the LORD, to do justice and judgment; **that the LORD may bring upon Abraham that which he hath spoken of him** (Genesis18:19 emphasis added).

---

[30]Elisabeth S. Dodds, "My Dear Companion," *Christian History,* vol. 4, no. 4, p. 16, as quoted in *The Family: God's Weapon for Victory,* Winepress Publishing, Mukilteo WA, 1995, p.351.

Also remember the blessing that would come when Abraham properly command-instructed his offspring

> ...*I will multiply thy seed as the stars of the heaven, and as the sand which is upon the sea shore: and thy seed shall possess the gate of his enemies: and in thy seed shall all the nations of the earth be blessed; **because thou hast obeyed My voice*** (Genesis 22:17-18, emphasis added).

The future of Christianity -- by God's plan and providence -- lies in the hands of those Christian parents who can successfully pass their faith on to *many* succeeding generations.

If you are ready to become a part of that future, you will want to read the next section which sets forth God's standards for training up children.

PART THREE:

GOD SETS THE STANDARDS FOR LIFE AND DISCIPLINE

The third point of the covenant concerns Law (*i.e.,* standards). Whether you want to build a skyscraper or just a shed for your gardening implements, you need a blueprint. When it comes to building the lives and character of His precious little ones, God does not leave us without plans. His Word supplies you with an inspired blueprint for training up your child.

The chapter **Truth in Labeling** will show you the parenting style prescribed by Scripture and how it depends on viewing covenant children from a Biblical perspective.

As you read **Strive Toward the Goal**, you will find your child-training objectives laid out from the Bible. Then you will discover a strategy straight out of Scripture that harmonizes with the Biblical parenting style discussed in the previous chapter.

A Doctrine of Discipline, as its name suggests, will give you the doctrinal foundation for spanking from God's Word. This includes an explanation from Scripture as to why and how the Holy Spirit uses *rightly applied* spankings to work repentance in your child's heart.

Truth in Labeling

How You Label Your Child in Your Mind Will Affect How You Train Him

For as he thinketh in his heart, so is he. Proverbs 23:7

1. Notice That It Makes a Difference

Ideas have consequences; beliefs drive behavior. You see this truth in action about you every day. After the terrorist attack of 9/11/01 many people stopped flying in airplanes because the event shook their faith in the safety of the airlines. Studies have shown that teachers will treat students differently according to the labels put on them by the school system (*i.e.,* "slow," "bright," "troubled," etc.). We should therefore expect the way we think about our children to affect how we train them.

Christian parent, how do you think of that little infant you cradle in your arms? What words do you use to describe that toddler of yours when you are talking to yourself? When you clear away all the hype and froth and pious-sounding verbiage that you may use in front of others, what words do you use to describe who your child is? Not everyone finds that question easy to answer. Let's help you find an answer by looking at some commonly-held beliefs about covenant children.

The first view we'll consider is that Christians' babies are **vipers in diapers**. Those who hold this view see their children as little pagans whose greatest need is conversion to Christ. Until the child professes faith, they hope to hold sin in check by strict discipline. The strength of this view is that it takes sin and the child's sin-nature seriously, but its weakness is that it down-plays the reality of the covenant promises we covered so fully in our study of the covenant in chapter two.

Another perspective -- related to the first -- is that the children are **vipers in covenant diapers**. People who hold this view still see the child as a pagan in need of conversion -- but they also say the child has great advantages as the member of a Christian [covenant] family (*i.e.*, the prayers of parents, hearing God's Word read and preached, etc.) This gives lip-service to the covenant and produces the surface appearance of taking God's covenant seriously.[31]

I present the third position as purely theoretical, because I know of no Christian who actually professes to hold it.[32] We might characterize it as the **angels in covenant diapers** outlook. These hypothetical folks see little need to impose any kind of discipline. They presume that their children will grow up to become faithful Christians without all that fuss and unpleasantness associated with child discipline. This notion seems to take the covenant seriously, but makes a mockery of it while it disregards the doctrine of sin.

The last position -- which I believe is the Biblical one -- I like to call the **babes in Christ** model. This means that by faith the parent considers his child to be a babe in Christ. When he does this, he treats sin seriously. Babes in Christ have much need for growth in sanctification. On the other hand, he also takes the covenant seriously. As long as the parent does his part -- even if his child does not yet show evidence of regeneration -- he rests in the assurance that God will fulfill His promise.

---

[31] I heard one adherent to the **vipers in covenant diapers** position say, "Being a child of the covenant is the next best thing to being saved." I replied, "That's like saying that going to Hell is the next best thing to going to Heaven."

[32] Although the way some believers conduct their child-training would seem to indicate that this is their position.

To see your infant children as **babes in Christ** is the natural outgrowth of embracing the Biblical teaching on the covenant that we have already noted. Many of you who read this will not be comfortable with this conclusion, but it is the Biblical and covenantal understanding of children. Some of you may have to overcome previous teaching in order to adopt the Biblical view.

Babes in Christ is the Biblical way for Christians to look at their children. If you want to raise your children Biblically, you need to embrace this truth as an unshakable conviction. Review **Life in the Covenant with Father**, if it's necessary. Prayerfully study the Scripture passages for yourself. Jesus says your children are such as make up the Kingdom of Heaven (Matthew 18:1-14; 19:13-15). If you fully concur with Him, you will more likely hold to your course.

2. A Critical Look at Parenting Styles

Now let's have a little fun with all of these different ways that Christians look at their offspring. We're going to put them together with different personal and stylistic preferences -- to come up with four different parenting styles. We'll use fictitious names to represent each style.

Drill Sergeant Dixie Plinn considers himself a realist. He does not believe in sugar-coating anything. He says, "I'll tell you just what my kids are: vipers in diapers...little sinners. And I'll tell you just what they need -- **Control**, and plenty of it, just like boot camp." His belief about his children dictates his approach -- imposing tough discipline.

On the other hand, Motivational Specialist I. Ken Dewit sees a different reality. He believes in the carrot rather than the stick. He says, "My children are flowers in the garden of God. As tender plants they need nourishment and lots of positive encouragement to grow up to their full potential." His basic view of his little ones leads him to offer them plenty of positive **Support**.

Workaholic Maya Jenduzz Fuller[*] rejects the perspectives of both Dixie Plinn and I. Ken Dewit. She sees children as self-sustaining, which fits her busy lifestyle She tells us, "Children are very adaptable. I have trained my own to be low-maintenance, although the time I *do* spend with them is *quality time*. Her opinion of children allows her to pursue her own interests, which gives her children **freedom from Support or Control**.

Finally, we come to a covenantal father named Christian Abrahamson, who sees his youngsters as **babes in Christ**. Because he knows they are sinners, he believes he must exercise **High Control** over them until they learn to control themselves. Because he also sees them as fellow Christians, he holds that he must give them **High Support** to aid their growth in Christ.

Application:
Some years ago a couple of graduate students did a research project involving the results produced by different parenting styles.[33] They tested a sample of students for their level of adjustment to life. They also polled the same students to find out the degree of support or control they received at home. They then divided the students into four groups -- according to the

---

[*] I couldn't resist the puns: Dixie Plinn = discipline; I. Ken Dewit = I can do it; Maya Jenduzz Fuller = my agenda's fuller.

[33] I learned about this research in a seminar session some years ago. Jim Berg, a faculty member at Bob Jones University, conducted the session. He did not give the source for this information in his lecture.

parenting styles that prevailed in their homes -- High Control/High Support (Christian Abrahamson); High Control/Low Support (Dixie Plinn); Low Control/High Support (I. Ken Dewit); and Low Control/Low Support (Maya Jenduzz Fuller). (See diagram 1.)

c - control s - support	S	s
C	**CS** Hi control/Hi support	**Cs** Hi control/Lo support
c	**cS** Lo control/Hi support	**cs** Lo control/Lo support

Diagram 1

The researchers found that the most well-adjusted subjects came out of homes that exercised both High Control and High Support. These people tended to have higher levels of self-confidence and more positive attitudes toward their future. They also manifested more mature attitudes regarding authority and their peers. It doesn't require a Ph.D. to see why.

At this point I need to clarify more fully the terms I have used in order to minimize any confusion. Here they are:
High Control - means that you demand strict obedience from your child as well as strict adherence to a precise and exacting code of conduct;
Low Control - by contrast, signifies that your parenting practices demonstrate lax enforcement and/or inconsistency in standards of obedience and behavior;
High Support - means you give abundant affection and encouragement to your child as well as appropriate recognition of accomplishments and good behavior;
Low Support - Low Support results from absence of emotional nurturing, often accompanied by harsh scolding or criticism.

Child development specialists have found that children need well-defined boundaries (both physical and behavioral) for their own peace of mind. Have you ever noticed a child in a wide open space seek out some nook or niche where he can feel safe and secure as he plays? When it comes to behavioral boundaries, his sin nature often conflicts with his need for security. Then he will test the bounds by disobeying.

The curious thing is that when his parents intervene with appropriate discipline and re-establish **control**, it restores his sense of safety and security. On the other hand, a child who successfully crosses a line of demarcation tends to feel insecure. He will often keep on pushing, just to see how far he can go before someone stops him.

I have seen this carry over into adult life when an individual whose lives an undisciplined life on the fringes of society goes out of control. He often seems relieved when uniformed police officers arrive on the scene. At that point he undergoes a complete transformation to become docile and cooperative (perhaps after token resistance). I think he does this because he knows the police are the only ones who will make him behave. Thus for many scofflaw adults, arrest by the police brings the only security they know.

In order to produce positive results in children, **support** must accompany **control**. Support in the form of praise and encouragement keeps control from becoming oppressive. Lack of parental support causes control to come across as harshly critical. This can provoke anger and discouragement in the child. It is probably for this reason that the second most well-adjusted group came from homes with High Support and Low control rather than the High Control/Low Support homes.

Many Low Support/Low Control homes in our society are homes in which the parents neglect their children. The families of alcoholics and drug addicts and those that for other reasons produce latchkey children all tend to fall into this category. Also, some parents think that "benign neglect" will make their offspring more independent. However, neglect is never benign, for children without anyone to care for them or about them will generally bring themselves up -- but not wisely or well.

Recap:

We have seen the four approaches to child-rearing, and we have noted the observations on what kind of children they produce. Even though the **High Support/High Control** approach grows out of a Biblical view of children as **babes in Christ,** we will continue to analyze it and the other styles by Holy Scripture. That is the topic of the next section.

3. A Biblical Look at Parenting Styles

At this point you have seen that the Biblical mindset which views your children as babes in Christ requires us to adopt the High Support/High Control style of parenting. Nevertheless, I want to take you to some specific Bible texts that speak to the various parental styles.

In the process of refuting the false styles you will see the truly Biblical parenting model confirmed. You will also find specific instruction on the the dangers involved in the nonscriptural styles and flesh out details that will help you to make the Scriptural style your own.

We can begin our Biblical examination with the parenting style that is easiest to discredit. That is the style we call **Low Control/Low Support**. As I see it, this is just another name for abandonment. Look at the following verse from Proverbs:

The rod and reproof bring wisdom: but a child left to himself bringeth his mother to shame (29:15).

The words "left to himself" represent a single word in the original Hebrew. The basic meaning of that word is to "send, send away, let go"[34] It is used in Psalm 81:12 where it refers to God's abandonment of Israel to its own desires and to the tragic outcome.[35] Obviously the Bible does not endorse the absentee parenthood of the Low Control/Low Support model.

Matthew Henry paints a repulsive picture of the Low Control/Low Support child in his comment on Proverbs 29:15.

*A child that is not restrained or reproved, but is **left to himself**,...to follow his own inclinations, may do well if he will, but, if he take to ill courses, nobody will hinder him; it is a thousand to one but he proves a disgrace to his family and **brings his mother. . . to shame**, to poverty, to reproach, and perhaps will himself be abusive to her and give her ill language. (emphasis in original)*[36]

I hope you can see why we ought to refer to Low Control/Low Support as a style of **non-parenting.**

See if you can guess which parenting style Paul warns us against in the verse that follows. In Colossians 3:21 we read,

Fathers, provoke not your children to anger, lest they be discouraged.

In order to understand this passage better, we will want

---

[34] R. Laird Harris, Gleason L. Archer, Jr., Bruce Waltke, ed., *Theological Wordbook of the Old Testament,* Moody Press, Chicago, 1980, p. 927.

[35] *ibid.,* p. 928.

[36] *Matthew Henry's Commentary,* MacDonald Publishing Co., McLean VA, Volume III, p. 960.

to look at how various men of God have understood it over time.

More than 400 years ago, John Calvin gave us the following observation on Paul's injunction against provoking children to anger:

> *He prohibits parents from exercising an immoderate harshness, lest their children should be so disheartened as to be incapable of receiving any honorable training....*[37]

Calvin is not the only commentator to see this verse as a ban on parental harshness. It seems that the American Puritan Matthew Henry agreed with Calvin. He made the following paraphrase of the Apostle Paul's words from Colossians:

> *Let not your authority be exercised with rigour and severity, but with kindness and gentleness, lest you raise their passions and discourage them in their duty, and by holding the reins too tight make them fly out with the greater fierceness.*

Notice that Henry uses the words "rigour and severity" instead of harshness, but the meaning is the same. He also said,

> *The bad temper and example of imprudent parents often prove a great hindrance to their children and a stumbling-block in their way.*[38]

I believe the words of Albert Barnes, pastor and commentator, will bring the application of this verse into full focus. He wrote,

> **Lest they be discouraged.** *Lest by your continually finding fault with them, they should lose all courage, and despair of ever pleasing you.*

Barnes continued,

---

[37] *Calvin's Commentaries,* Baker Books, Grand Rapids, 2003 (reprint), Volume XXI, "Epistle to the Colossians," *William* Pringle, tr. p. 220.
[38] *op cit., Volume VI,* p.766.

> *Children should not be **flattered**, but they should be **encouraged**. They should not be so praised as to make them vain and proud, but they should be commended when they do well.* (emphasis in the original)[39]

At this point I'm sure you have figured out that the Apostle Paul's admonition against provoking children warns us against the parenting style we have labeled High Control/Low Support. The Biblical testimony is opposed to parents whose control is accompanied by harshness rather than by tender affection.

Since you know that Holy Scripture condemns Low Support, you might consider adopting the Low Control/High Support style of parenting. After all, according to the researchers it produces the second most well-adjusted children. And it sounds a lot easier than trying to be always in control of your children.

As you read the folowing passages, however, you will see that the Bible definitely advocates high parental control.

> *Proverbs 19:18 -- Chasten thy son while there be hope, and let not thy soul spare for his crying.*
>
> *Proverbs 22:15 -- Foolishness is bound up in the heart of a child; but the rod of correction shall drive it far from him.*
>
> *Proverbs 23:13-14 -- Withhold not correction from the child: for if thou beatest him with the rod, he shall not die. Thou shalt beat him with the rod, and shalt deliver his soul from hell.*

Use of a rod is the the most severe form of control the Bible allows a parent to exercise. There's no doubt that rod-based correction involves a high degree of control.

---

[39] *Barnes' Notes on the New Testament,* Kregel, Grand Rapids, 1966 (reprint), p.1075.

Recap:
Our brief look at Scripture has shown that three of the parenting styles are unbiblical. That leaves one parenting style yet to discuss, which I shall do in the next section.

3. The Biblical Model for Parenting

From the ground we've already covered, you might use the process of elimination to conclude that High Control/High Support is the Biblically-based parenting style. We should base our teaching, however, not just on what the Bible forbids, but on what it commands. Just to make sure, then, let's look at another passage -- one that shows us the style which is the proper model for Christian parenting.

Take a look at Ephesians 6:4.

> And, ye fathers, provoke not your children to wrath; but bring them up in the nurture and admonition of the Lord.

The whole clause *bring them up in the nurture and admonition of the Lord* overflows with significance regarding parenting styles.

E.K. Simpson interprets "the nurture and admonition of the Lord" in a way that lends general support to our High Control/High Support view of parenting.

> *The father as the paterfamilias is singled out by the apostle for admonition. His sway must comprise a **positive** and **negative** element, a blend of firmness with gentle treatment. (emphasis added)*[40]

We can easily comprehend control as a negative element and support as a positive element of

---

[40]*The New International Commentary on the New Testament: Ephesians and Colossians,* E. K. Simpson (Eph) and F.F. Bruce (Col), Wm. B. Eerdman's Publishing, Grand Rapids, 1972 (1957), p. 136.

child-rearing. But in order to know that this was the intent of Paul -- and God -- we need to understand more precisely the language of the phrases **"bring them up"** and **"nurture and admonition"**.

John Calvin casts significant light on the words "bring them up".

> But Paul goes on to say, "let them be fondly cherished;" for the Greek word...which is trans-lated **bring up**, unquestionably conveys the idea of gentleness and forbearance.[41]

He also comments,

> Kind and liberal treatment has rather a tendency to cherish reverence for their parents, and to increase the cheerfulness and activity of their obedience, while a harsh and unkind manner rouses them to obstinacy, and destroys the natural affections. (emphasis in original)[42]

Here, as in Colossians, we find strong evidence for High Support in parental relations to the child.

Calvin also shows that the passage teaches us the necessity for parental control.

> To guard them, however, against the opposite and frequent evil of excessive indulgence, he again draws the rein, which he had slackened, and adds, "in the instruction and reproof of the Lord." It is not the will of God that parents, in the exercise of kindness, shall spare and corrupt their children. Let their conduct towards their children be at once mild and considerate, so as to guide them in the fear of the Lord, and correct them also when they go astray. That age is so apt to become wanton, that it requires frequent admonition and restraint.[43]

Thus you can see that the decree to *bring up* our

---

[41] *op. cit.*, "Epistle to the Ephesians," p. 329.

[42] *ibid.*, p. 328.

[43] *ibid.*, p. 329.

children contains within it a strong argument for the High Support/High Control style. Even so, we have not plumbed the depth of meaning in Ephesians 6:4. Let's examine the words *nurture and admonition* to see what more this passage has to teach.

The word rendered *nurture*[44] could easily be translated as *child discipline.* In fact, it contains the Greek word for child in it. Hebrews 12:5,7,8 & 11 uses *chastening* to represent this same term (the related verb *chasten* appears in verses 6, 7 & 10). In that context it obviously refers to spanking, which is the strongest form of parental control.

The word translated "admonition"[45] in Ephesians 6:4 means counsel by the use of words.

> *[I]t is the training by word -- by the word of encouragement, when this is sufficient, but also by that of remonstrance, of reproof, of blame, where these may be required; as set over against the training by act and discipline....*[46]

Thus verbal support and control both find expression in the Biblical term admonition.

Recap:
Now let me sum up the words found in Ephesians 6:4. The word translated *nurture* actually refers to physical discipline: spanking. This reference to strong control is bounded on one side by *bring them up,* a term that carries the ideas of gentleness and cherishing. On the other side we find *admonition,* which signifies the use of words both to support (encouragement) and to control (warning, blame). We must conclude that the Apostle

---

[44]Greek, *paideia.*

[45]Greek, *nouthesia.*

[46]Richard Chenevix Trench, *Synonyms of the New Testament, ninth ed.,* London, MacMillan and Co., 1880, p. 112.

Paul meant to strongly urge his readers to exercise both **High Support** and **High Control** in rearing their children.

4. The Parental Office

> And ye fathers, provoke not your children to wrath: but bring them up in the nurture and admonition *of the Lord* (Ephesians 6:4, emphasis added).

The Biblical teaching that your child is a babe in Christ determines the proper parenting style -- High/Control & High/Support. The label *babe in Christ* also points back to a vital truth mentioned in the first chapter. You must always keep it in mind that **Your child belongs to Christ**, not to you.

The pagan cultures of Greece and Rome held that parents owned children as chattel. Fathers could exercise their authority to sell or kill their children, and their society would not challenge them. Our postmodern humanist society, on the other hand, says that the child belongs to himself. This idea of ownership opens the door for the state to intervene any time it judges that the parent has violated the child's rights.

You see the importance of settling the matter of who owns your child. If you allow your thinking to be tainted with even the tiniest leaven of pagan, humanist ideas, it will affect how you perform as a parent. Therefore I urge you to conclusively reject both the notion that you own your child or that your child owns himself.

Your authority is that of someone appointed by Christ to protect, and guide His child. The authority is real because you act as the covenantally designated representative of the Lord Himself. But the fact that you represent Him also puts limits on your authority -- you must bring up your child in the nurture and admonition **of the Lord.**

Note: For further study into the status of covenant children please read "One Bread, One Body" in the book *Feed My Lambs* by Tim Gallant (Pactum Reformanda Publishing, Box 23009, Grande Prairie AB, Canada T8V 6X2.)

Strive Toward the Goal

But First You Have to Know Where You're Going

1. The Goal of Child Training

In life -- as on the rifle range -- if you aim at nothing, you'll hit it every time. Therefore, in order to successfully bring up your children, you need to know what the bullseye looks like. We can see from Scripture that the goal for children is the same target we should all be shooting for.

> Till we all come in the unity of the faith, and of the knowledge of the Son of God, unto a **perfect man**, unto the measure of the stature of the fulness of Christ: **that we henceforth be no more children**, tossed to and fro, and carried about with every wind of doctrine, by the sleight of men, and cunning craftiness, whereby they lie in wait to deceive; but speaking the truth in love, may **grow up into Him** in all things, which is the Head, even Christ...(Ephesians 4:13-15, emphasis added).

The goal for every Christian is to become a *perfect* [*i.e., mature*] *man.* American culture in its last days may glorify perpetual adolescence, but the Biblical standard is mature adulthood. The preceding passage also points out the standard or measure of maturity: *the stature of the fullness of Christ.*

The Lord Jesus Christ, in His humanity, embodies human nature at the pinnacle of its development. Christ's mind -- His thoughts, attitudes, character and wisdom -- and His behavior show us what a truly grown up human being looks like. We are not, however, limited to the Gospels as we focus on Christ as our standard.

All God's Word reveals to us Christ, the Mature Man. The Law reveals to us the bedrock of His character; the

Psalms give us a glimpse at the breadth and depth of His passion; the historical books show us something of the carefulness of His preparation. All His Word is the standard by which you and I measure our maturity, because it all reveals something of Him.

Ephesians does more than reveal that Jesus is the measure of maturity. It gives an important rule of thumb you can use to measure your children's progress in growing up -- as well as your own. This is not a substitute for the fullness of adulthood found in Christ, but a prime sign that one is developing in Him.

The sign the Apostle speaks of is that from now on we "be no more children, tossed to and fro by every wind of doctrine...." In other words he says that the **stability** (no more tossed to and fro) which comes through **discernment** (by every wind of doctrine...whereby they lay in wait to deceive) is a major signal that one is leaving childishness behind.

Paul started the passage we are studying by telling us that Christ is the *standard* of maturity. He then told us that stability through discernment is the *sign* of maturity. Now let's see what he says about the *speech* of maturity.

> But speaking the truth in love [we] may grow up into Him in all things, which is the Head, even Christ: from whom the whole body fitly joined together and compacted by that which every joint supplieth, according to the effectual working in the measure of every part, maketh increase of the body unto the edifying of itself in love (Ephesians 4:15-16).

Note that "speaking the truth in love" accompanies growing up in Him in all things. This is not the same thing your mother meant when she told you, "If you can't say something nice, don't say anything at all." That's just the starting place. Paul's emphasis is not on what you *don't say*, but on what you *do say*.

The mature Christian must not only refrain from saying unkind, crude or selfish things. He must also learn to speak the truth in love. He does this so that he may participate with his Lord in the body's *edifying itself in love.*

In a nutshell, that's exactly what you should aim for in rearing your child. Of course, none of us has attained that full level of perfect maturity yet -- not you, not I, not even the Apostle Paul in his lifetime (see Philippians 3:12-14). But if you are to lead your child to maturity, you too must *press toward the mark.*

2. The Strategy for Attaining the Goal

In his letter to the churches of Galatia, Paul uses the illustration of a father's design to bring his son to maturity to portray the relationship of the New Covenant to the Mosaic Covenant. Although the apostle's main point centered on the covenants, his illustration provides us with the Biblical strategy for bringing up children.

> But before faith came, we were kept under the law, shut up unto the faith which should after-wards be revealed. Wherefore the law was our schoolmaster to bring us unto Christ, that we might be justified by faith. But after that faith is come, we are no longer under a schoolmaster (3:23-25).
>
> ....
>
> Now I say, That the heir, as long as he is a child, differeth nothing from a servant, though he be lord of all; but is under tutors and governors until the time appointed of the father.
>
> Even so we, when we were children, were in

79

bondage under the elements of the world: but when the fulness of the time was come, God sent forth his Son, made of a woman, made under the law, to redeem them that were under the law, that we might receive the adoption of sons. And because ye are sons, God hath sent forth the Spirit of his Son into your hearts, crying, Abba, Father. Wherefore thou art no more a servant, but a son; and if a son, then an heir of God through Christ (4:1-7).

In Israel's childhood the Law served as a *pedagogue* to bring them to Christ.

The pedagogue or tutor, frequently a superior slave, was entrusted with the moral supervision of the child. Thus his office was quite distinct from that of the [teacher]...[47]

The Mosaic Law imposed external control on every aspect of the Israelite's life in order to show him his need for the grace of Christ. Just as a pedagogue imposed total external control over a child until he saw the need to exercise inward control.

For the Israelite who looked forward to Christ and for the covenant child, the objective is the same. Someone takes control of him until by grace through faith the Holy Spirit begins to form the character of Christ within him. This Spirit-wrought character forms the basis of self-control. And self-control -- temperance -- is the fruit of the Spirit (Galatians 5:22-23).

In the chapter **Truth in Labeling** we saw that your babe in Christ needs high support and high control. At first, you the parent apply that control externally and totally. As the child grows toward maturity, the high degree of support and encouragement continues. But

---

[47] *The Epistle of St. Paul to the Galatians,* JB Lightfoot, Zondervan Publishing House, Grand Rapids, reprinted 1974, p. 148.

the discerning parent will gradually relax control as his child grows in grace and develops his own discernment accompanied by self-control through the Spirit's work directly in his heart and indirectly through you. (see Diagram 2).

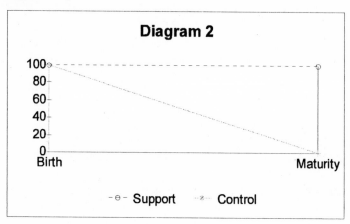

Diagram 2

As you come to grasp God's wisdom in this plan, you will see how it applies to Paul's instruction in Ephesians and Colossians. He has much to say to the adult believers throughout both epistles. To the children, however, he simply instructs them, *obey your parents.* Obedience -- submission to parental control -- is the foundation for all else the Holy Spirit will accomplish in the life of your covenant child.

This means that obedience must comprise the first and most fundamental lesson that you teach your son or daughter. Apart from this basic training, everything else you do with and for your child is unsure. The certainty of the covenant promise hinges upon your successfully asserting your parental authority in such a way that your child voluntarily submits.

The early stages of training a child to obey often shapes up as quite the battle of wills. And make no mistake, a battle it is -- a battle against the flesh for the soul of your child. You cannot win it in your own strength, but in the power and wisdom of God's Holy Spirit. But with determination and God's help, you can gain control for your child's own sake -- and yours.

The sad fact is that if you do not exercise control over your child, your child will probably wind up controlling you.

> *As for My people, children are their oppressors,*
> *and women rule over them. O My people, they*
> *which lead thee cause thee to err, and destroy the*
> *way of thy paths* (Isaiah 3:12).

You can find these poor folks everywhere, and you've seen them as well as I. The mother with her child in the shopping cart...the child demands some trinket or treat...mom says no...child puts up a noisy, ugly fuss...mom furtively glances around her, embarrassed by the scene ...then she caves in.[48]

If that mother is a Christian, she is on the way to losing the battle for her child's immortal soul. And you will lose, too, if you think you can depend on methods alone to raise up your child. We will cover Scriptural methods of discipline in the next chapter -- but even with the Bible's own methods, success depends on your prayerfully entering into the process in partnership with the Holy Spirit. And remember -- you're the *junior* partner.

While we're on the subject of obedience, I want to point out God's standard for obedience. The Lord of heaven and earth does not accept anything less than 100% obedience. If He is the model, you will accept no less from your child. You must raise your own expectations

---

[48]Sometimes she compounds the problem by promising her little dear something even bigger and better if he/she will only cooperate.

for your children from obeying 50% or 75% of the time. You should expect them to obey you the first time every time you give them a command [within the bounds of Biblical ethics, of course].

3. Keep the Goal Before You

The battle ahead is hard, especially in the first two to six years. That is why it's important to keep the strategic objective in sight. As difficult as your child may seem, and as hard as it is to make him obey, the fruit of it all will be a lifelong relationship with a mature, godly person you've helped to disciple.

Don't feel that your need to keep reviewing the goal somehow suggests that you are especially weak-willed. God put us together as goal-seeking creatures. Jesus Himself kept His goal in view as He entered the struggle for our redemption.

> Looking unto Jesus the author and finisher of our faith; Who **for the joy that was set before Him** endured the cross, despising the shame, and is set down at the right hand of the throne of God (Hebrews 12:2, emphasis added).

Let me say that whatever the difficulty you endure in training your child to obey, the rewards far outweigh the cost. By the time each of my children were seven, I had forgotten the last time I had to spank them. I don't want to say that my offspring are typical -- yours may require a longer training period, or a shorter one.

But although following the Biblical strategy starts out hard, at some point it gets easier. On the other hand, you may try to find an easy way out and avoid taking the initiative in the battle of wills. Then, sooner or later your child will bring the battle to you. What seemed the easier way gets progressively harder, and in a worst case scenario, your child goes to hell.

One somewhat irritating side effect of training your children in obedience early will come when you are enjoying the result of cheerfully obedient children. The frazzled parents of disobedient children will say something like, "Sure it's okay for you -- you have easy children."

The choice is yours: **hard at the beginning** or progressively **harder all the way through.**

Note: If you would like to look into developing more discernment, I recommend that you read *A Call for Discernment* by Jay Adams, Timeless Texts, Woodruff, SC, or www.timelesstexts.com/.

A Doctrine of Discipline

You Can Know from the Bible How Spanking Will Help Your Child Spiritually

1. The Foundation for Discipline

We need to make sure that our convictions concerning discipline are rooted deeply in God's Word. First, because every aspect of the Christian's life -- down to spanking a misbehaving child -- needs to be grounded in the Word of God. In addition to this, administering the rod correctly (and for the right reasons) is the most difficult part of parenting, as far as I'm concerned. Furthermore, the climate of opinion in twenty-first century humanist society sets itself against parents who use physical means of discipline. For all these reasons you must establish your convictions on nothing less sure than the Word of the Living God.

For the historical beginning of disciplinary punishment we look back to our first parents in the garden. God warned Adam and Eve of what would happen if they ate from the one tree symbolizing Him as the source of knowledge and morality. After they disobeyed, the Lord sought them out and pronounced judgment.

The sentence of judgment included a life of hard labor, eviction from the garden and eventual physical death. This first disciplinary action recorded in the Bible came in answer to sin. Adam and Eve directly disobeyed God, and He punished them for it. You must punish your disobedient child for the same reason that God punished Adam and Eve -- disobedience is sin.

Scripture makes it plain that a parallel exists between God and fathers in their discipline.

> *Thou shalt also consider in thine heart, that, as a*
> *man chasteneth his son, so the LORD thy God*

chasteneth thee (Deuteronomy 8:4).

And ye have forgotten the exhortation which speaketh unto you as unto children, My son, despise not the chastening of the Lord, nor faint when thou art rebuked of Him.

For whom the Lord loveth He chasteneth, and scourgeth every son whom He receiveth. If ye endure chastening, God dealeth with you as with sons; for what son is he whom the father chasteneth not? But if ye be without chastisement, whereof all are partakers, then are ye bastards, and not sons. Furthermore we have had fathers of our flesh which corrected us, and we gave them reverence: shall we not much rather be in subjection unto the Father of spirits, and live? For they verily for a few days chastened us after their own pleasure; but He for our profit, that we might be partakers of His holiness (Hebrews 12:5-10).

We can see here that God is the standard and pattern for perfect discipline. He *always* disciplines His children for their own good. Fathers in the flesh do not always measure up to that standard. Still, God remains as the standard, so you should strive to discipline your children for *their* good, not for selfish reasons.

We can see another reason to strive to administer discipline as God does. In His covenant with David He said,

*I will be his Father, and he shall be My son. If he commit iniquity, I will chasten him **with the rod of men, and with the stripes of the children of men*** (II Samuel 7:14, emphasis added).

Here God promises David that He will use men to discipline his offspring. God appoints certain people to carry out the chastening necessary in the lives of His people.

In Ephesians 6:4 we see that God appoints fathers in particular to discipline children of the covenant.

And ye fathers, provoke not your children to

wrath; but bring them up in the nurture and admonition of the Lord.

In a previous chapter we pointed out that the word translated *nurture* in this verse is translated *chasten* in Hebrews 12. Therefore in this verse God pointedly commands Christian fathers to administer physical discipline to their children.

Indeed, God considers the duty to discipline your child so crucial that He put the following statement in the Book of Proverbs:

He that spareth his rod hateth his son; but he that loveth him chasteneth him betimes (13:24).

The physical aspect of discipline is so important to your child's training in obedience -- so pivotal to his spiritual and eternal well-being -- that God says if you neglect it, your actions say you **hate your child**. Now, that's strong language, so I want to relate an experience that may shed some light on this difficult concept.

Soon after my first child's birth I became an observer of children. I wanted to see how they behaved and how their parents acted upon or reacted to their behavior. The incident that turned me into an avid child watcher occurred in the home of Dave and Jodi,[49] friends of ours.

Dave had a full plate -- he pastored a church, held down another a full time job, and he also served as director of a small Christian camp. Dave and Jodi practiced hospitality with an open door policy. They also had three children of preschool age.

One afternoon Laura and I sat on the couch in Dave and Jodi's living room. Dave was talking on the telephone to a board member about camp business

---

[49]Not their real names.

Three year old Johnny came out of the children's play room with a ball about the size of a volley ball. He began to bounce and throw it around the room.

The ball lightly bumped Dave's leg. He turned from the phone to admonish Johnny that he should throw the ball only in the play room. Then his attention went back to the phone conversation. What happened next branded itself upon my memory because it unfolded so clearly that I could see exactly what was happening.

Little Johnny stood still across the room from his dad. You could almost see the wheels turning as he studied his father -- evaluating. "How busy is Dad? Will he back up what he just said?" Then he continued bouncing and throwing the ball just as before.

Johnny's ability to gauge his father's attention proved accurate. Dave went on talking, blind and deaf to his son's disobedience. And, as we shall see later, this kind of defiant disobedience is exactly the behavior which requires a spanking, according to Biblical standards. Johnny continued until the ball hit a lamp, almost knocking it over.

Dave then swatted Johnny on the bottom (a mere token spanking) to start him on the way to the play room. "I told you to take that ball into the other room." Johnny stomped out of the living room in obvious anger without any sign of sorrow for his disobedience.

I began to evaluate the little drama that had unfolded before me. I asked myself, "Now, just exactly what did Johnny learn from this experience?" The answer: he learned that his father responded to being provoked rather than to actual disobedience. He also learned that he could get away with an outburst of anger in response to his father's correction.

Some might think that the ability to work around his parents as he did might make Johnny happy. After all, he was learning to read the signals from his parents that would eventually enable him to do exactly as he pleased. On the contrary, Johnny demonstrated all the signs of a very unhappy, troubled little boy.

We lost track of Dave and Jodi for several years. But evidently Johnny grew into a troubled and angry teenager. At the age of twenty he ended his own life. The message he received from his father's inadequate discipline was not that his father loved him. It doesn't matter what Dave's feelings were toward his son, for love includes a whole lot more than feelings alone.

Love is an inner attitude that produces a specific set of outward behaviors (see I Corinthians 13). Love requires a conscious commitment that makes a priority of the loved one. Sadly, Dave did not demonstrate behavior that showed love toward his son. ...*[H]e that loveth him* **chasteneth him betimes**. Betimes means right away (*i.e.*, as soon as the child disobeys).

Please learn from Scripture and from Dave's tragic example. Don't hate your child. Love him enough to follow the Lord's example in discipline. Love God **and** your child enough to act as God's appointed representative in the discipline of His covenant little ones.

Recap:
Sin is the root cause of a child's disobedience. God first exercised punitive discipline over Adam and Eve after their first disobedience. God serves as the pattern and example for parents in discipline. God requires that parents in general - and fathers in particular - exercise physical discipline over their children. Proper application of the rod is a strong sign of parental love.

2. What Spanking Teaches and Why It Works

The rod is the Biblically sanctioned implement for administering a spanking. It will communicate certain lessons to your toddler long before you can make an impression on him with appeals to reason.

> *In the lips of him that hath understanding wisdom is found: but a rod is for the back of him that is void of understanding* (Proverbs 10:13, emphasis added).

Children start out pretty much void of understanding. If you wait to begin training them in obedience until you can hold an intelligent conversation with them, it will be too late.

As soon as your child has enough understanding to do what you tell him[50], you must train him to do so **the first time, every time.** Consistent and proper application of the rod will teach the following lessons:

1. Ethical cause and effect - immediate discipline will teach a young child that bad behavior produces bad results. This will lay a groundwork for learning to fear God, long before he can grasp the awful reality of hell;

2. The meaning of *repentance* - a toddler will learn to repent of disobedience long before he intellectually comprehends the word in terms of its Biblical and theological content (see below);

3. The high value of obedience - a very young child trained to obey will accept it as a high priority matter in his life;

---

[50]This requires great discernment on your part as a parent. Truly defiant behavior generally appears in the "terrible twos." Between the ages of one and two a parent will want to begin asserting authority and eliciting obedience, as children at this age show a remarkable geniality -- the "winsome ones".

4. Respect for parents - a youngster who is made to obey will display respect for your authority, which takes the hassle out of getting him to accept your standards later;

5. How to live peaceably in society with parents, brothers and sisters, and playmates - this is the foundation for all social interaction later;

6. Security and happiness in the love and care of his parents - the disobedient child demands his own way, which makes him unhappy and oblivious to his parents' acts of kindness;

The fundamental lessons your child learns from obedience training while he is still void of reason will accompany him throughout his life. They will also form an indispensable core for learning more challenging concepts later on.

At this point you may be wondering why the rod makes such an effective tool in molding the young mind and spirit. The Bible, of course, has an answer for that question. At the same time Scripture will help us to understand something about an observation that social "scientists" have made concerning development of values.

Those who do research in social psychology say that by the age of two a child has formed his basic understanding of what the world is like. At this age the child's experience has provided him with a fundamental perception of the "normal". He will judge to be wrong anything that does not conform to his concept of the normal. We can say that at this stage his standards have a definite shape, like jello that has set in a mold.

Then at about the age of ten or so, something further takes place. At this stage the child's basic values crystallize -- they harden **for life**. Some churches which require a profession of faith from children for church membership have conducted surveys which tend to verify these observations. The age period from ten to twelve marks a sharp drop-off in professions of faith. If they have not professed faith in Christ by that time, it becomes much less likely that they will ever do so.

Even though spiritual change comes more painfully in adulthood, God shows us that such a thing is possible. And *how* it is possible. In his Second Epistle to the Corinthians the Apostle Paul speaks about the emotional turmoil caused by his first letter.

> For though I made you sorry with a letter, I do not repent, though I did repent; for I perceive that the same epistle hath made you sorry, though it were but for a season. Now I rejoice, not that ye were made sorry, but that ye sorrowed to repentance: for ye were made sorry after a godly manner, that ye might receive damage by us in nothing. For **godly sorrow worketh repentance to salvation** not to be repented of: but the sorrow of the world worketh death (7:8-9).

Scripture here informs us that **godly sorrow works repentance to salvation**. Interestingly, social "scientists" have also observed that an emotional crisis can often serve as the catalyst for change in an adult's value system.

The passage in II Corinthians is not the only one that seems to confirm this. James associates emotional crisis with repentance as well.

> Draw nigh to God, and He will draw nigh to you. Cleanse your hands, ye sinners; and purify your hearts, ye double minded. Be afflicted and mourn and weep; let your laughter be turned to mourning, and your joy to heaviness (4:8-9).

Although this passage addresses adults, we have no reason to believe that this concept does not apply to children as well.

We do in fact find another association between a negative emotion (grief) and spiritual change in Hebrews 12:5b-11.

> My son, despise not thou the chastening of the Lord, nor faint when thou art rebuked of Him: for whom the Lord loveth He chasteneth, and scourgeth every son whom He receiveth.
>
> If ye endure chastening, God dealeth with you as sons; for what son is he whom the father chasteneth not? But if ye be without chastisement, whereof all are partakers, then are ye bastards, and not sons.
>
> Furthermore, we have had fathers of our flesh which corrected us, and we gave them reverence: shall we not much rather be in subjection unto the Father of spirits, and live? For they verily for a few days chastened us after their own pleasure; but He for our profit that we might be partakers of holiness.
>
> Now, no chastening for the present seemeth to be joyous, but grievous: nevertheless afterward it yieldeth the peaceable fruit of righteousness unto them that are exercised thereby.

We know that *chasten* -- child-train -- as used in this passage emphasizes the physical side of discipline because it appears as a counterpart to the word *scourge* -- whip -- in verse six. Here it refers to God's use of physical hardships to discipline believers -- His children. We can apply these verses to our own disciplinary practice because, as we observed earlier, the passage also draws a parallel between the chastening of earthly fathers and the chastening of our Heavenly Father. Then it goes on to say that this discipline is not joyous, but *grievous*.

The word translated *grievous*[51] here is the same word

---

[51] *lupe*

used to speak of that *sorrow* which works repentance in II Corinthians 7:8-9. Such grief-producing discipline, Hebrews 12:11 tells us, yields *the peaceable fruit of righteousness to them which are exercised thereby.*

Can we really transfer this spiritual precept to human child discipline? If so, then the parent who administers the rod **in a godly way** acts as God's agent to introduce **godly sorrow** into the child's life. He does this in the faith that godly sorrow will eventually produce **repentance to salvation** as well as the signs that accompany salvation: **the peaceable fruit of righteousness.**

Proverbs 23:13-14 seems to validate our conclusion.
> *Withhold not correction from the child: for if thou beatest him with the rod, he shall not die. Thou shalt beat him with the rod, and shalt deliver his soul from hell.*

Deliver his soul from hell -- the word rendered *hell* in the Old Testament is also sometimes translated *the grave* as a euphemism for death. In this passage, if it means *grave* -- *death* -- the sense does not change, for the grave and death are more-than-symbolic representations of God's judgment. To deliver a child's soul from hell or the grave or death speaks of delivering him from the judgment of God. We call this deliverance salvation.

I do not mean to imply that one spanking will necessarily result in repentance to salvation. If you consistently apply the rod, however, you should confidently expect that the Holy Spirit will be working with you to change your child's heart. When that change finally occurs, the peaceable fruit of righteousness should not be far behind. And then the war of wills that characterizes the early years will cease.

Conclusion

Now we see a key portion of the mechanism which God intends to use to fulfill the covenant promise. He will work through those believers who as His agents use Scriptural discipline. Specifically, the Holy Spirit uses the rod to produce godly sorrow, which in turn leads to repentance and the peaceable fruit of righteousness. That brings us to the question of how to administer discipline in a godly way, which we shall cover in the next chapter.

PART FOUR:

GOD PRESCRIBES

LIFE-CHANGING DISCIPLINE

The fourth point of a Biblical covenant contains sanctions (or penalties). In Part Three you saw that godly sorrow works repentance and that God uses parents as His agents to introduce godly sorrow into a sinning child's life by way of the rod. In Part Four you will see how to apply the rod.

In **Giving Godly Spankings** you will read about how you must prepare your own heart before you should administer discipline. You will also find a Biblical standard for determining what behavior you should punish with the rod as well as a description of the spanking process drawn from Scriptural precepts.

You may especially want to read **Is It Ever Too Late?** if you picked up this book as the parent of an older child. It will direct you back to the basics, and it will suggest how you may want to apply them in your situation.

Giving Godly Spankings

How to Apply the Rod in a Scriptural Way

I have always hated spanking my children. No Christian with normal feelings likes to inflict pain on anyone, especially his own family. My own preferences notwithstanding, I have spanked my children because God has appointed the rod as the proper means to train children in righteousness.

This chapter deals with the practical application of Scripture to the spanking itself. I warn you that some of the subject matter is as distasteful, and as unpleasant as it is necessary to effective, godly spanking. Also, keep in mind that the discipline of the rod should take place in the context of an encouraging, loving, high support family.

1. Prerequisites for Godly Spanking

Motive. The question that must always be on your mind in the disciplinary process is, "Why am I spanking my child?" Many things your child does will make you angry, but anger is the worst motive for a parent to spank a child. In the Epistle of James we read,

> Wherefore, my beloved brethren, let every man be swift to hear, slow to speak, slow to wrath: for the wrath of man worketh not the righteousness of God (1:19-20).

For me, one of the hardest parts of disciplining my children was to set aside my anger. It is easy to show your anger by yelling or through harsh words, but the Scriptural standard is to control your children with dignity (I Timothy 3:4).

If you do not control your angry words, then sooner or later you will not control your actions. A parent who has lost control of himself has no business picking up a rod (or anything else) to spank his children. If you have trouble controlling your anger, I recommend you find a pastor specifically trained in the Biblical style of counseling called *Nouthetic Counseling*[52].

Once you have settled the matter that you will not let anger motivate your discipline, you will be able to concentrate on your child's obedience rather than your feelings. This however, raises another question: what is your motive in wanting obedient children? God resists the proud, but He gives grace to the humble (James 4:6). Do you want your children to be good for your own glory or God's?

The years that I spent teaching in Christian schools opened my eyes to parental motives. Some parents truly wanted a Christian education for their children. Other parents had a different motive: **respectability.**

The latter group of parents wanted their children in an environment where they would be less apt to get involved in drugs or some other activity that would bring shame to the family. They feared the opinions of men. Now it's good to want to keep your children off drugs. But if you want it just to keep your standing in the community, that's a poor motive.

The parents motivated by respectability also seemed to suffer a nagging fear: the fear of Christianity itself. They did not want their children to become radically Christian. It would not do to have an oddball in the family who practiced his faith all day, every day. As long as their sons stayed off drugs and their daughters did not become pregnant, they were getting what they

---

[52]Secular counselors deal with behavior, but not with the root cause: sin.

wanted from the school.

Before you even think about picking up the rod of correction, you need to think about what you want from child discipline. I hope you will discipline your children because you want them to grow up as assets to Christ's kingdom -- strategic weapons in God's war against the prince of darkness. If you've had the motivation to read this far into this book, it's probably a pretty good sign that your heart is in the right place.

Humility. By humility I mean, first of all, willingness to submit to God's discipline in your life. We've discussed Hebrews 12:5-11 which speaks of God's chastening in our lives to produce the peaceable fruit of righteousness. We cannot expect God to bless and work through the discipline we give our children if we rebel against His discipline.

To submit to God's chastening you will need to develop the habit of keeping your conscience clear. This means confession -- both to God and to any other person you've wronged -- and making amends, where necessary. If you're like me, this will not come easily. That's why you need to look back to your *motives* -- and to remember that the eternal souls of our children hang in the balance. While we're on the subject of confessing and asking forgiveness, we need to talk about an application that hits much closer to home.

In addition to showing humility by confessing to God and your neighbor, you will need to practice humility in another way. You must confess to your children when you wrong them -- and ask for their forgiveness [This really goes contrary to my natural man.]

My natural man tells me that to admit that I'm wrong to my children will constitute a show of weakness. God's

Word, though, says "Confess your faults one to another" (James 5:16). Well, I'm one, and my child is another, so I guess that verse applies here. One of my own failures in this area may help you to grasp the importance of lowering yourself to the point of making a confession to your children.

I can recall one time when I was going through a period of acute discouragement for my inability to properly provide for my family. My attitudes and subsequent decisions caused even greater hardship for my wife and children. One of my daughters -- then in her teens -- suffered particularly from my insensitivity to my family during this time. I told her that **if** I had offended her in any way, I was sorry.

Months later, after things had returned to a more normal state, my daughter confronted me. She said, "Daddy, you said that **if** you had offended me, you were **sorry**. You brought me up better than that." To my shame, I knew just what she was talking about.

I had always taught my children not to hide behind words like **if** and **sorry** when they confessed their faults. They were to tell how they had wronged the other person and then say, "I was wrong. Please forgive me." In my pride I tried to hide from my responsibility for the grief I had caused. My daughter knew better than to be fooled by my insincerity.

I then made a proper confession to my daughter. I thank God that she had learned the lesson of humility well enough to remind her father in one of his lapses. If you've ever experienced the frustration of a boss or a teacher who could never admit it when he was wrong, you know how my daughter felt.

Your children will react the same way to you, unless

you learn to humble yourself and ask their forgiveness when you...

display inappropriate anger...

break your word...

say something hurtful...

do something that makes for a poor example...

or in any other way wrongfully cause grief, pain, discouragement, etc.

It takes humility to admit to a three-year old that you were careless and did not get home in time to take him to the park. Then it takes the grace of God to ask him to forgive you. Nevertheless, I hope you will take encouragement from my experience and observations.

I have found my own children quite ready to forgive me, even from the youngest age. On the other hand, in the aforementioned Christian school, I encountered many students who would not only refuse to forgive, but would attempt to exploit the one who asked, because they took confession as a sign of weakness. As I listened to them talk, and as I got to know their parents, I came to a conclusion regarding this attitude.

I concluded that the students who would not graciously forgive came from parents who either saw asking forgiveness as a sign of weakness, or who used guilt as a means of punishment. If you withhold forgiveness as a punishment to your children, then they will not learn to forgive you or others. My "Christian" students had never learned how to ask for or grant forgiveness at home. Their parents had missed the prime opportunity to teach their children, a key concept of the

Christian faith --forgiveness.

Many times and in many ways we all give offense. Each occasion provides an opportunity for us to exercise humility by asking forgiveness. Each occasion also presents us with an opportunity to teach our little ones as we ourselves grow in Christ.

Discernment. I recommend that every expectant father and mother take steps to begin to develop discernment before their first child is born. You cannot effectively discipline without some awareness of what your child is up to. Otherwise you will let too many of his sins slide by and/or punish innocent behavior.

For example, you *should apply the rod* when your youngster stubbornly refuses to do what you say. On the other hand, what if he has a hearing problem...? You can see how you **must** have enough discernment to tell when apparent disobedience really stems from another cause. Other causes can vary greatly.

You may need to separate a good motive from a bad consequence -- as when your toddler wants to surprise you by clearing the table...and breaks your heirloom serving platter. Or you may just need to ask yourself if your child has enough command of language to understand the order you just gave. Sometimes you have to discern who is the truly guilty party in a dispute between children - or even between your child and an adult.

On one occasion some neighbor children accused my daughter of a now-forgotten transgression. She denied that she did it. The children's mom intervened and said that she had seen the whole thing and that my daughter had indeed committed the act in question. My daughter still maintained her innocence.

The act itself would probably have drawn no more than a stern warning not to do it again. But my little girl received a spanking from my wife for lying. Afterward, she still tearfully protested her innocence. Years later the matter came up in conversation, and she said that she had received unjust punishment.

I believe her. You see, my gut feeling at the time was that my daughter had been telling the truth. I must plead guilty to fear of contradicting another adult. This was in spite of the fact that I knew that the neighbor lady and her husband practiced dishonesty in other matters. And in spite of the fact that her manner and facial expressions made me suspect she was lying.

Skewered on the prongs of indecision, I failed to intervene on my daughter's behalf. You too will fail in the area of discernment from time to time. But take heart, because it will provide yet another opportunity to grow in humility as you ask your child's forgiveness.

One more critical area will require discernment on your part. You will need to acquire a knack for separating immature behavior from sinful behavior. As the Apostle Paul observed,

> When I was a child, I spake as a child, I understood as a child, I thought as a child... (I Corinthians 13:11).

The childhood mental immaturity Paul describes (which includes untrained judgment) goes hand-in-hand with undeveloped physical attributes.

Youngsters spill things, drop things, bump into things and make a myriad or other blunders without intent or malice. The same behavior in an adult might signal a spirit of defiance and rebellion. But in a child it may simply mean that he has not yet developed the fine muscle control necessary to the task at hand. The difference between developmental immaturity and rebellious behavior, however, is not always crystal clear.

Because of the difficulty in distinguishing childish behavior from sin, I recommend that a parent not overburden his child with expectations. In the early years, especially, limit your use of the rod to the times that your child disobeys a clear command you have just given.

You will likewise not do well to use spanking to deal with childish irresponsibility. A child of six or seven who forgets his chores or neglects to wash his hands before a meal needs reminding, not spanking. Some matters may call for you to set up a system of rewards and losses to enforce mature, responsible conduct. In any case we shall see in a few pages why you should limit the rod to cases of direct disobedience.

Before we move on, I would like to say a word about potty training. I have firm convictions against using the rod to enforce toilet training. Children seem to display a wide latitude of ages when it comes to readiness for this milestone. I know how anxious it makes Mom when junior does not seem inclined to use the commode. It would make her job so much easier if she and Dad could just force him to use the bathroom!

Please do not succumb to the temptation. Toilet training -- as with bedwetting -- requires the utmost patience and understanding on the part of parents. To spank a child for these problems before he develops the awareness and ability to comply will only foster indignation and bitterness on the part of your child.

Recap:
Godly and effective physical discipline requires a

parent to approach the task with the right **motives**, with **humility** and with **discernment**. This list of prerequisites is not exhaustive, for training a child is part of life, and life comprehends all that God does for our salvation and sanctification. Nevertheless, this short list is a good place to start.

2. Behavior That Begs for the Rod

Although I touched on it in the last section, I want to elaborate here on what behavior demands a response from you that may include a spanking. Let's start by looking a couple of verses from Proverbs.

> *Judgments are prepared for scorners, and **stripes for the back of a fool*** (19:29, emphasis added).

> *A whip for the horse, a bridle for the ass, and **a rod for the fool's back*** (26:3, emphasis added).

The words translated *fool* in the Bible do not refer to someone with limited mental capacity. The Biblical fool has committed himself to oppose the character and precepts of God's Law (Proverbs 1:7, 22; 14:9). He is a moral rebel.

Now notice that we **control the horse** with a whip, and we **control the donkey** with a bridle. Therefore this verse leads us to the conclusion that the way to **control a moral rebel** is with the rod. You use the rod on your children for the same reason -- **control** -- when they exhibit a spirit of rebellion by directly disobeying you or your spouse. You do this because they have rebelled against God's appointed authority in the home: Dad and Mom.

In Proverbs 22:15 we find a Scripture that makes the same application.

> *Foolishness is bound up in the heart of a child, but the rod of correction shall drive it far from him.*

The word for *foolishness* here is actually a stronger term than the word for *fool* in the verses quoted at the beginning of this section. The word carries the idea of insolence in the face of moral authority. This insolent attitude leads to disobedience. When you spank your son or daughter for disobedience, you are initiating a process that will eventually drive insolent foolishness from his heart. Therefore defiant and disobedient behavior is the primary behavior that demands the rod in response.

Notice that this dovetails exactly with what we learned in chapter four about a child's primary duty. In that place we quoted Ephesians 6:1.

> Children, obey your parents in the Lord: for this is right.

If the first duty of children is **obedience**, then by reasoning backwards, we come to very same teaching that we find in Proverbs. That is, we must use our most powerful and effective means of discipline against **dis**obedience. Hence, in order to fulfill your duty as a parent, you must spank your child when he disobeys.

3. The Physical Aspects of a Spanking

First of all, I want to deal with the instrument used to spank and the area of application. The Bible repeatedly speaks of the rod as the instrument of choice for spanking (see above). You cannot go wrong if you just follow these directions of Holy Writ literally. Still, in order to understand the rationale of the rod, let's review just what you expect the spanking to accomplish.

As you spank, you want to inflict enough pain to cause an emotional crisis that leads your child to godly sorrow, which in turn will produce repentance (see chapter 5). Most pain receptors in the body are relatively close to the surface of the skin. Therefore it is possible to inflict enough pain to bring about grief and sorrow without causing grave harm. Remember, the need here is for *physical pain, not serious injury.*

Several years ago I remember hearing about a religious community that made headlines in the news media after a boy died from complications as the result of a spanking. The leaders of the community urged the parents to beat the boy, who exhibited willful, defiant behavior. The leaders and/or the parents made two thoughtless, stupid mistakes that ultimately proved fatal to the youngster.

First of all the parents administered the spanking with a heavy bat, rather than a rod. A thin rod causes stinging pain without necessarily producing the deep tissue injuries associated with a baseball bat. A bat can actually produce serious injury without smarting as much as the rod. Second, the parents spanked the boy through his diaper.

A thick layer of cloth can muffle the effects of a blow to the surface of the skin, while allowing the damaging force to pass more deeply. In other words, the parents disciplined their son under the *exact opposite conditions* that a spanking calls for. They caused maximum deep tissue damage to their son with a minimum of pain.

They continued the spanking because he still would not submit. The boy died from complications arising from the fact that his parents had turned his buttock muscles to jelly. I relate this horror story in order to stress that since those folks didn't understand the Bible's command to use a rod, they shouldn't have modified it.

Even when we *think* we understand, we should probably not try to improve on God's standard. I know a young couple who use a wide, heavy strap to spank their son. The husband made it from a discarded conveyor belt at the place he worked. He understands the need for a spanking to cause pain. And he testifies to the fact that the strap really stings.

This same man has told me that he thinks his son doesn't respond to spankings as he ought. It is as though the boy has developed some level of immunity to the spanking. I tried to tell him to use a rod, as the Bible says. He responded by saying, "Just smack this strap against your leg. See how it stings!"

Yes, the strap stings **over a broad area**, and that is just the problem. After a few blows the nerve endings become less sensitive to the stimulus. Subsequent blows don't hurt as much, so the boy never reaches the desired point of emotional crisis.

A rod, on the other hand, strikes a much narrower area. With a rod, you would find it hard to strike the exact same place twice in a row. The nerve endings do not become numb from overstimulation, and the child suffers enough pain to bring on the emotional crisis. We never know too much nor grow too wise to trust the Bible in a simple thing.

The Bible does not give us exact dimensions for the rod, but I recommend that it not exceed a quarter, or maybe three eighths of an inch, tops. Anything bigger starts to have the effect of a bat. If you use a wooden dowel from the hardware store, a smaller diameter will tend to break too easily. Rather than buy a dowel, some do-it-yourselfers may want to go to the tree in their yard for a rod.

If you cut your own switch from the branch of a tree, the green wood will not break so easily. Just be sure it does not exceed the dimensions I gave above. Also, you'll need to remove any knots, bumps or protrusions from the exterior. I stress this, because it's important that you minimize physical damage, even as you seek to maximize the superficial (surface) pain.

As to the physical area of application, the Bible does not say exactly where to spank a child, but I'm a traditionalist -- with good reason. Again, let's return to the objective of a spanking. We want an area of the body away from vital organs, with plenty of pain receptors, which is not easily subject to serious injury. The buttocks fits all of these requirements. You can call it the *derrière* or the backside, if you please. But as far as the anatomy of a spanking is concerned, our search bottoms out here.

4. The Stages of Rod-Based Discipline

Now I want to take you through the process of a godly spanking. There is such a thing as an ungodly spanking. Which kind of spanking you end up giving will depend to some degree on how well you integrate the following Biblical stages into your procedure. The procedure I lay out takes certain universal Scriptural precepts and applies them to the corrective process[53].

Stage One: Doctrine. The word *doctrine* in the Bible denotes more than theological teaching. It includes the concept of *precept* or *commandment* -- *i.e.,* moral instruction. Godly discipline begins right here, with clear instruction.

My son, keep thy father's commandment, and

---

[53]I did not originate the four point outline: doctrine, reproof, correction, instruction in righteousness; it comes from II Timothy 3:16. Both Bill Gothard and Jay Adams have used it to describe the stages in godly change.

forsake not the law of thy mother: bind them continually upon thine heart, and tie them about thy neck. When thou goest, it shall lead thee; and when thou awakest, it shall talk with thee.

For the commandment is a lamp; and the law is light; and reproofs of instruction are the way of life (Proverbs 6:20-23)

A clearly understood command will serve as the fundamental building block of character which lasts a lifetime. As profoundly important as it is, such a command may come out of your mouth as an extremely mundane-sounding order.

For example, you see your two-and-a-half-year-old son reaching for a lamp that he might knock over and break. You say, "Neddy, don't touch that lamp." This is a clearly stated command.

When Neddy pretends not to hear you and continues to reach out for the lamp, you are ready to enter stage two of the disciplinary process.

<u>Stage Two-A: Reproof.</u> *Reproof* as we use it here signifies that you are about to put your child to a *test.* Make no mistake about it, you are being tested, too. Do not make the mistake of many a parent who commands a youngster, "Don't do that," and then turns back to a conversation without monitoring the child's obedience. So, let's return our focus to Neddy.

In spite of clear instruction, Neddy has started to disobey you. Hopefully, you have positioned yourself to nip his misbehavior in the bud. Take Neddy's hand in mid-reach -- grasp it firmly, but not roughly. Then make eye contact and say, "If you touch the lamp, I will spank you." Say it clearly, firmly and without the tinges of anger or irritation you may be feeling at this point. (Following a plan like this one may help you to mimimize anger, even if you don't eliminate it entirely.)

110

Then let go of his hand and wait for his reaction. If he goes back over to his blocks to play, thank the Lord for an easy victory [this time]. On the other hand, he may decide to see if you mean what you say. In this case, as soon as his hand makes contact with the lamp, physically intervene once again.

I cannot overemphasize the need to issue a direct and unmistakable warning. This draws the line in the sand. When the child crosses it, the time for a spanking has come. He knows it, and you know it. No doubt in anyone's mind. This will save you from the trap of bluffing -- repeated warnings with no follow-up. The following story will serve to warn you against the error of using a bluff to try to bring your child to compliance with your commands.

Some twenty-five years ago, I knew a couple with two boys, about twelve and ten years of age. The wife was a bluffer, and the boys knew it. She would tell the boys to do something, and I could see from their reaction that they had Mom figured out. They knew that she would continue to nag and threaten until she became really angry. Only then would she act.

These boys knew exactly the point at which their mother would become angry enough to punish them. This made possible a little game they liked to play. It was called, "Let's take Mom to the edge and see how long we can keep her there." During the summer and on weekends they could delay obeying in some matters and misbehave in others so as to keep Mom dancing on the edge all day long.

This went on long enough until one afternoon she was driving her boys in the car. Her youngest sassed her without realizing how close she was to the breaking point. She stopped the car, and hit him in the mouth, as she screamed profanities at him. Then she said, "I am going to take you home, and when we get there I'm going to get your father's gun and blow your brains out."

Thankfully, she did not make good on her promise. But at that moment she did realize that something was terribly wrong with her disciplinary method. She had, in fact, trained her sons to control her through their misbehavior. All this came about through delaying action after drawing the line. Remember this Scripture?

> He that spareth his rod hateth his son: but he that loveth him chasteneth him betimes (Proverbs 13:24).

Betimes means *at once* or *right away*. Dragging out the warning phase of the discipline process only wears on everyone's nerves. You show your love to your child by drawing the line and then taking immediate action when he decides to cross it. Now we may return to Neddy and the point where he has crossed the line.

At this point, do not issue any more warnings. He has disobeyed, and now you must deal with it. You will ask him the question, "What did you do?" Not, "Did you...?" but, "What did you do?" This lays the groundwork for him to learn to confess his sins.

Do not let lack of an answer stop the process. As the child learns to recognize the process, you should train him to confess his disobedience. "I touched the lamp." At this point you move directly to Stage Two-B (below).

Sometimes your child will defy you without directly disobeying you. "Neddy, don't touch the lamp." A surly Neddy stomps back over to where his toys are. This display of anger is as much a challenge to your authority as direct disobedience, so you need to draw a line for this behavior, as well.

Again, firmly but calmly: "Come back here, young man. [He comes.] Now, walk back over there, and if you stomp your feet again, I'll give you a spanking." At this point Neddy rolls his eyes in disdain, but walks back without stomping. Do you call him on his facial expression? Definitely!

The Bible tells us,

> The eye that mocketh at his father, and despiseth to obey his mother, the ravens of the valley shall pluck it out, and the young eagles shall eat it (Proverbs 30:17).

> For they are impudent children and stiffhearted Ezekiel 2:4).

Impudent means hard-faced. God associates the impudent expression with a stiff heart that does not respond to verbal warning and rebuke. So, let's keep the figurative ravens and vultures away from Neddy's eyes by administering discipline to him on the basis of his defiant facial expressions.

Develop a mindset that never sees sin as *cute*. Have you ever noticed one of those parents who just can't help but laugh at their little urchin's sassy words or behavior? One couple we knew had a little girl of about three years of age who was adorable -- and she evidently knew it. Sometimes when an adult was talking to her, she would dismiss the older person with a saucy turn of her head. Then with her nose in the air, she would walk away "in a huff." Her parents either did not notice this behavior or just accepted it. Other adults laughed at how cute she was. But at three she was practicing an attitude that could become a way of life. **Rule of thumb:** if you don't think that it would be cute if your neighbor's barbarian teenager did it, it's not really cute when your little cherub does it, either.

<u>Stage Two-B: Reproof.</u> Once you catch Neddy in the act of disobeying, you need to send or take him to a

113

private place. Following the pattern of dealing with an offending brother (Matthew 18:15-17) as well as the injunction to control our children with dignity (I Timothy 3:4), spankings should take place between you and your child alone. An audience will only complicate matters.

Compose yourself as you make your way to the room where you intend to spank Neddy. I have repeatedly emphasized controlling your anger in all these stages because you do not want Neddy to learn to read and respond to your level of anger rather than to your plain command. Remember,

> *Wherefore, my beloved brethren, let every man be swift to hear, slow to speak, slow to wrath: for the wrath of man worketh not the righteousness of God (James 1:19-20).*

After you have Neddy in private, let him know that you are going to spank him. Also let him know that you are just carrying out God's orders to you. "You know, Neddy, if I don't spank you, God will have to punish me for not doing my job." You may not say this every time, but be sure the child understands that you, the parent are acting as God's agent.

Now put Neddy in a position where you can keep control of him and where you will not suffer injury from any kicking or flailing that he does. Also, make sure that no diaper or heavy clothing comes between his bottom and the rod. Now strike his bottom repeatedly with the rod. This brings us to a crucial question.

"How long shall I continue the spanking," you ask? You can gauge that by listening to his cry. Children cry differently depending on the cause. The first several times you strike Neddy's buttocks with the rod, you're liable to hear an angry, protesting type of cry. Don't stop yet, because if you do, all you will have accomplished is provoking him to wrath, and remember what Paul said in Ephesians 6:4:

> And ye fathers, provoke not your children to wrath; but bring them up in the nurture and admonition of the Lord.

I've seen parents give six or seven quick swats, then send their angry toddler off to sulk and brood. If you stop in the midst of his angry outcries against your discipline, you will give his flesh the victory and harden him in his rebellion.

Therefore, you must have the endurance of will to keep on spanking until Neddy's cry becomes the weeping of a broken heart. Susannah Wesley said she spanked her children until they cried softly (you'll know it when you hear it). This is crucial, and I know it's not easy.

I've caught a glimpse of myself in the mirror more than once as I spanked one of my children. Words like *bully* and *brute* sprang to my mind as I saw a 200+ pound man spanking a little child with a rod. At these moments you need all the courage of your convictions that you can muster. That's why I laid the groundwork in the early chapters. You need the unwavering conviction that you are acting for the eternal benefit of your child.

If you have properly prepared your heart and planned your words and actions, you are showing compassion, not brutality in spanking Neddy until his angry cries have passed. Take courage from the following verse.

> Chasten thy son while there is hope, and let not thy soul spare for his crying (Proverbs 19:18).

If you have what it takes to bring your child to this point, you have done him a great favor.

Proverbs 20:30 tells us,

> The blueness of a wound cleanseth away evil:

so do stripes the inward parts of the belly.

The verse is saying that the blows of the rod actually cleanse a festering conscience. From this point on, things get better quickly. Move on to the next stage.

<u>Stage Three: Correction.</u> Here *correction* means restoring Neddy to his correct place. It means raising him up in the humility of his repentance and restoring him to your full fellowship and approval. You do this by taking him quite literally up into your arms with full forgiveness, comfort and love. ***The parent who spanks should also be the one to comfort.*** Assure Neddy that you love him. If he has truly reached the point of brokenheartedness, he should willingly receive and give affection.

Avoid preaching, moralizing or revisiting his sins. Your scolding cannot improve upon the lesson you have taught him with the rod, and you don't want him to think that you have not forgiven him (and if you haven't forgiven him, **you** need to repent). You may want to remind him that Jesus loves him and died on the cross so that he could have his sins (not just his guilty conscience) cleansed. While his heart is still tender you will want to move him into stage four.

<u>Stage Four: Instruction in Righteousness.</u> Now is the time to direct Neddy to ask forgiveness from anyone else he has hurt or offended in his disobedience. He can also make simple restitution such as cleaning up a mess he made, giving one of his toys in exchange for the playmate's toy he broke, etc.

Now Neddy's participation in family life will go more smoothly -- for a while. Then his sin nature will reassert itself, and you'll be off on another round of godly, rod-based discipline. Don't forget that these bouts with

Neddy's sinful will should take place in the context of a home where both parents offer plenty of love and support at all times. High support and high control is the Biblical standard (see chapter 4).

Also, don't forget that you're not wrestling primarily with flesh and blood. The battle is spiritual, so prayer is in order. Ask God to send His Holy Spirit to strengthen you and to work the work of regeneration in your little Neddy or Nadine's heart. That's the real objective, here. Only God Himself can change the human heart and produce that peaceable fruit of righteousness.

It may take one, two, three or four years, but don't give up. A time will come when your child will not push past the warning stage. Then after a while he will obey as soon as you give the command -- the warning will not be needed.

Once you see the peaceable fruit begin to appear in your child's life, the necessity for spankings will become fewer and farther between and finally become altogether unnecessary. You will inherit the blessing of a peaceful relationship with your son or daughter. At that point you will be able to concentrate your efforts on **discipleship**, the most truly exciting and rewarding aspect of child training.

A word of caution: We live in a postchristian society that not only frowns upon the methods of discipline described in this chapter, but cherishes a deep hatred for the objective of training up faithful Christians as well. Please use all care not to do lasting harm to your child. Also use discretion in situations where neighbors might see a mild bruise on your child's buttocks and report you to a child service agency. In many a locale an accusation is as good as a conviction.

A Disclaimer

Nothing I have written in this chapter (or anywhere else) should be construed to advocate any manner of child punishment other than the use of a light rod on the child's buttocks with only such force as will cause no serious or lasting injury.

Punching, kicking, biting, or the shaking of a child are totally inappropriate, as are striking the child's face, twisting its limbs, the use of sharp or jagged objects, or the use of boiling water or hot objects to burn a child. These and other injurious practices are signs of an adult who is out of control. If you or anyone you are acquainted with has ever done any of these things, please seek counsel from a pastor qualified in the field of Nouthetic Counseling. For more information about Nouthetic (*i.e.*, Biblical) Counseling, contact:

Christian Counseling & Educational Foundation
1803 E. Willow Grove Ave., Glenside PA, 19038
Telephone: 215-884-7676 Website: www.ccef.org/

Is It Ever Too Late?

For Parents Who Have Older Children

This chapter is for those parents who already have older children, and who previously had never heard anything like the message of this book. You thought that it was the norm for your children to grow up constantly at odds with your parental authority. You took your experience and the experience of the people you know as the measure of "normal" Christian teen (and pre-teen) behavior. Now you realize as you cope with trying to control a rebellious teenager (or prodigal adult) that the message of this book has come too late.

"If only ..." are words of regret we have all spoken as we view our lives with 20-20 hindsight. But sad as it is, you can't change the past. When we dwell on past failures, we tend to focus on placing blame. That's always been such a tendency of mine that around our house, we've made a joke of it. After any mishap when someone says something like, "I'm sorry," or, "It was my fault," then someone else will invariably say, "Well, at least we know whom to blame ... and that's the important thing."

When you focus on fixing blame, you are not focusing on fixing the problem. That is one reason that confession of sin is important to the human mind. Confession not only removes the roadblock between the sinner and God, but also removes the roadblock of self-blame that keeps a man or woman from taking positive action. Therefore confession to God will give you a new start in dealing with your problem. It will also put you and God back on the same side in the matter.

So, the way to overcome self-blame is to acknowledge

that you are worthy of blame. Just do it once and for all in prayer to God. Even if you didn't know about the Biblical standard of high support and high control, or the doctrine of discipline, you can confess it as a sin of ignorance[54]. Once your conscience is clear, you may still grieve over your straying child. But you will also be able to focus your thoughts and prayers on winning him back, and that's *really* the important thing.

After confession comes the active pursuit of your goal. The basics have not changed, though their application has. We begin with God.

1. God Still Sets the Agenda

When God told Abraham to offer up Isaac on the altar, Abraham had to change his expectations. He had to give up his own agenda for the son of promise. At that point God put him at the crossroads of deciding who would ultimately be in charge of the young Isaac. The crisis of a rebellious child has put you at the same crossroads.

You now have the opportunity to offer up your child to God in prayer. Can you tell God from your heart that you are willing for Him to set the agenda for your son or daughter? This is not easy to do with someone you love, for God's agenda for restoring a stray one may involve bringing that one to ruin in order to bring him to his senses. Which reminds me of something that took place several years ago.

A young couple was having some difficulty, and rather than work it out, the husband abandoned his wife. The husband's parents realized their son was in the wrong, and together with the wife, they prayed for the hus-

---

[54]Many equate ignorance with rudeness; here I mean it as *unawareness*.

band's return. The young man's mother approached me with some concern about these prayer sessions.

The mother told me, "My daughter-in-law keeps praying, 'Lord, put him flat on his back, if that's what it takes.'" She continued, "But I don't want to see my son flat on his back." Knowing the wife, I'm sure there was some vindictiveness in her prayer. I don't remember exactly what I told this troubled mother, but now -- twenty-five years later -- I think I know what I *should* have said.

Today, I would tell that woman, "Your daughter-in-law should be willing to pray, 'Put **me** flat on **my** back, if that's what it takes.' You -- the mother -- are the one who should be willing to say, 'Put my son flat on his back, if that's what it takes.'" You see, the wife's willingness for God to punish her husband had nothing to do with sacrifice. The mother's willingness for God to punish her son would have had everything to do with sacrifice.

I remember a certain company whose customer service department distributed a pin to their reps. It simply said, "Whatever It Takes." That was Abraham's attitude when God told him to sacrifice Isaac. That needs to be your attitude before God, about bringing a loved one back into the fold.

2 You Are Still God's Appointed Agent

We have already seen that God has appointed fathers and mothers as His covenantal representatives with respect to their children. An older child who lives in your home and eats at your table is still under your covenantal authority. The Lord has commissioned you to represent Him to your children. That gives you a ready answer when your teenager asks, "Who gave

121

your the right to tell me what to do?"

God Himself gave you not only the right, but the responsibility to guard your children from sin and to guide them into righteousness. Let this fact give you courage and confidence in the extremely hard task of dealing with your disobedient older child. He aims his challenges to your authority like an arrow to destroy your confidence, and with it, your determination to make him do what is right.

Resolve from this moment on to act in good conscience as God's agent for the eternal well-being of your child.

3. Obedience and Mature Christian Character Are Still the Standards To Which He Must Conform

Earlier in the book we saw that the first lesson a child must learn is obedience (Ephesians 6:1). That obedience becomes the groundwork for building mature Christian character in the image of Christ (Ephesians 4:13-16). Although it will be much harder to bring about compliance at this stage, the standards remain the same.

When dealing with rebellion, you find that when you're not managing a crisis, you're anticipating the next one. As the sign says: "When you're up to your hips in alligators, it's easy to forget that your original objective was to drain the swamp." But you must not forget. No matter how chaotic it gets, you must always fix your eyes upon the Word that defines the goal and sets the standard.

4. Godly Sorrow Still Works Repentance

In chapter six we saw that *godly sorrow works repentance* (II Corinthians 7:8-9). We used that truth to explain why spanking works. Now let's remember that

Paul wrote those words, not to children, but to adults about their own repentance. This is basic to the way God put you and me together. The basics have not changed just because your child is older.

It may not be appropriate -- or possible -- to take him over your knee for a spanking. But the truth remains that godly sorrow works repentance. How you apply this truth differs as to whether you're dealing with a young child or a teenager, and even moreso when you're dealing with an adult child. Nevertheless, just as surely as sin brings judgment, the sorrow associated with that judgment is basic to repentance.

Acting as God's agent you spank disobedient toddlers. With older preteens and teenagers you will want to work out a system of consequences for disobedient and rebellious behavior. Spell out the rules as well as the disciplinary penalty to your youngster: Tell him, *"When you do this, here's what will happen."* Post a chart on the back of his bedroom door, so there will be no mistake about what you require of him. Here we go back to instruction: making the rules clear (see Stage One of Rod-Based Discipline in chapter 6

After you've done that, read the book of Proverbs many times and pray for the wisdom of Solomon. I can almost guarantee that more than one situation will arise to sorely test both the rules you have made and your will to enforce them. Through it all, remember that your standard is justice according to God's Word, not fairness according to your child or his friends (or even your own understanding).

With an adult child who has chosen to live apart from God, you cannot impose rules with penalties. Yet you still have some degree of covenantal responsibility. And where God gives responsibility, He also grants authority.

For an example from Scripture we can look to the Book of Job.

> And [Job's] sons went and feasted in their houses, every one his day; and sent and called for their three sisters to eat and to drink with them. And it was so that when the days of their feasting was gone about, that Job sent and sanctified them and rose up early in the morning, and offered burnt offerings according to the number of them all: for Job said, It may be that my sons have sinned and cursed God in their hearts. Thus did Job continually (1:4-5)

Job took his covenantal role seriously enough to offer sacrifices on behalf of his grown sons and daughters, *just in case* they had sinned.

Fathers today do not stand in the same patriarchal position as Job. But the covenantal link still exists between a father and his grown sons and daughters. This gives you leverage on a plane that your unregenerate child wouldn't understand.

You can and should pray to the Lord in your official capacity as covenant head. As an appointed official who comes before a Great King, you need to plead for God's work in your child's life . Don't just wing it -- plan and present your case to God. Then watch carefully to see what He brings to pass.

The Lord will probably answer your prayer by bringing *sorrow unto repentance* into your adult child's life. You will need great wisdom and restraint as you deal with this troubled one. You must resist the parental urge to rush in and position yourself between your prodigal and the consequences of his sin.

In the Parable of the Prodigal Son, the offender did not repent until he was penniless and without a roof over his head. His love of pleasure eventually led him down to the point where he *came to himself.* Interestingly, most sins carry the seeds of judgment in them. Your own rebel's transgressions may, in God's providence, bring him to the end of his rope, so that he will really confront himself and his sin. He can't do that if you always stand by to rescue him from the "spanking" which God has arranged for him.

On the other hand, don't make the mistake of saying, "I told you so," or "See, that's what you get for not obeying God." You cannot succeed if you try to nag your older child to Christ. Not only does it not work, it will drive him farther away. Instead, you must walk a narrow road where you avoid badgering him without giving approval to his bad behavior (I know -- easier said than done). Perhaps it will help if you take a lesson from dog trainers and the Prodigal's father.

When training a dog not to eat anything except what the owner gives him, trainers do something quite instructive. The owner stays out of sight and the trainer hides with a BB gun. A piece of meat is left where the dog will find it. When the dog finds it, the trainer shoots the dog in the hindquarters with the BB gun. Now comes the interesting part.

As soon as the dog "yips" in pain, the owner appears and begins to comfort the dog. As they repeat the process over the next few days, the dog associates pain with taking unauthorized food, while he identifies comfort with his owner. Now, I'm not suggesting that people are on the same level as dogs, but I do find a parallel between this training technique and the behavior of the Prodigal's father.

We find no record that the father lectured, preached, nagged or harassed his son in any way. Rather he let the *reproofs of life* do their work in the young man's heart. Then when the lad returned, the father did not say, "I told you so," but went out to meet him with a welcoming and comforting embrace. You can apply this lesson to your own situation.

If your prodigal comes to you with a need, empathize. Tell him you're praying for him, offer to set up an appointment with your pastor -- who hopefully has some knowledge of Nouthetic counseling. You can offer any kind of help or encouragement as long as you do not consent to relieve his pain apart from his repentance. This means tactfully saying things like, "I'd give you money if I thought it would help, but you need to take care of the root cause of your money problems."

A child in sin might react against such a suggestion, but as long as you do not speak in anger or bitterness, you can probably keep the lines of communication open. Since I've just mentioned pastoral counseling, I would like to say a word or two about your greatest earthly resource.

In terms of earthly authority the pastor and elders of your local church are the big guns in your struggle with a rebellious child -- especially those still living in your home. Read this somber passage from Deuteronomy:

> If a man have a stubborn and rebellious son, which will not obey the voice of his father, or the voice of his mother, and that when they have chastened him, will not hearken unto them: then shall his father and his mother lay hold on him, and bring him out unto the elders of his city and unto the gate of his place;
>
> And they shall say unto the elders of his city, This our son is stubborn and rebellious, he will not obey our voice; he is a glutton, and a drunkard. And all the men of his city shall stone him with stones, that he die: so shalt thou put away evil

from among you; and all Israel shall hear and fear
(21:18-21)

Note that the rebellious son of this passage is no toddler. The sins mentioned are the sins of an adult or a near-adult. Also understand that I am not suggesting that your church should put incorrigible teens to death.

Nevertheless, the passage not only reveals to us how God views rebellious youths, but it also tells us that a parent who has trouble controlling his older children can appeal to his elders for help. Some people will say that since the passage refers to the elders of a city, it means that parents should go to the civil government for help -- in other words, state social services. We need to recognize, though, that under the Mosaic Covenant, we do not find a distinct line drawn between civil and church power. Moreover, the Body of Christ is the City of the New Jerusalem (Hebrews 12:18-24; Revelation 21:9-10).

The elders of your local church are elders in the City of God. That means that after you have dealt with a child who lives in your home -- or who is on his own (if he is still a church member)-- you can begin the process of church discipline. When I say *church discipline*, however, please understand that I mean a lot more than just meting out punishment.

The first objective and the best outcome of church discipline is the correction of the offender, followed by reconciliation and restoration. Note that this does not differ from the objective of rod-based discipline. But when the elders become involved, we see discipline raised to a wholly different level. You will have help and participation by your spiritual shepherds in working out the solution of your problem. Beyond that, your child will have to face the fact that his rebellion is not his own private affair.

Look at the procedure for discipline set forth by the Lord Jesus.

> *Moreover, if thy brother trespass against thee, go and tell him his fault between thee and him alone: if he shall hear thee, thou hast gained thy brother. But if he will not hear thee, then take with thee one or two more, that in the mouth of two or three witnesses every word may be established. And if he shall neglect to hear them, tell it unto the church: but if he neglect to hear the church, let him be unto thee as an heathen man and a publican. Verily I say unto you, Whatsoever ye shall bind on earth shall be bound in heaven; and whatsoever ye shall loose on earth shall be loosed in heaven (Matthew 18:15-18)*

The last verse above should give you some idea of the awesome judicial authority given to the church by our Lord.

If the avenue of church discipline looks like a possibility for you, I would recommend that you obtain a copy of *Handbook of Church Discipline* by Jay Adams.[55] He gives great insight into the process, and how to conduct each step Biblically.

I have only scratched the surface here of how you may face the difficult task of seeking to win an older child to Christ. No discipline is easy or pleasant. My prayer for you as I write this is that God may grant you the endurance and the fortitude to do what is right in all things.

5. The Results Are Still by God's Grace

God explicitly promises that a covenant child properly command-instructed from the earliest age by his

---

[55]Timeless Texts, 88261 Highway 73, Suite B, Stanley, NC 28164, phone: 800.814.1045, toll-free, www.timelesstexts.com

parents will persevere in the faith. I do not see an equivalent promise that a parent may claim on behalf a child with whom he started too late. Many factors enter in, and even if I knew them all, this book would not be the place to discuss them.

However, our God is the God of all grace. He has saved you and me by His grace. As the parent of an older rebellious child, you can do no better than to cast yourself and your child upon His mercy.

PART FIVE:

ONLY GOD'S GRACE

GUARANTEES THE RESULT

The fifth point of a Biblical covenant spells out the various provisions for succession to covenant authority and inheritance of covenant blessings. For your children this means faith in Christ that produces eternal life as testified by the peaceable fruit of righteousness as well as adult status with both the privileges and the responsibilities of establishing their own Christian families.

In the final chapter, **Discipling for Destiny**, you will find some general rules and practical suggestions for the most interesting and most fulfilling role that you as a parent will occupy: preparing your children to succeed you in the covenant leadership roles of husband [or wife] and father [or mother].

Discipling for Destiny

How to Turn Your Children into Followers of You and Your Lord

And He ordained twelve that they should be with Him.
Mark 3:14

Some who read this come from backgrounds that encourage the evangelism of children from Christian families to insure that each one will have a conscious conversion experience. Others pray that their children will never know a time that they did not know the Lord. Whichever tradition you come from, if you practice godly discipline, you will come to a point where the contest of wills has ended. You will know a blessing that many parents don't dare to believe possible.

Instead of facing off on opposing sides, you and your children will know the blessing of being on the same team. Of course you have always been for them, but now they will also be for you. This doesn't mean there won't be bumps in the road. But you'll both be on the same road, traveling in the same direction. You will be their guide for this part of the journey.

1. You Are the Curriculum as Well as the Teacher

Once you have passed the difficult task of training your child to obey, and after you begin to see the peaceable fruit of righteousness begin to appear, then you will enter into a new phase of relationship with your child. Like Solomon you will be able to say,
> My son, give me thine heart, and let thine eyes observe my ways (Proverbs 23: 26).

Your ways are more than what you do. They are those inner workings that make you who you are. When you have your child's heart, your ways will become to him

131

the model for normal living. This is the essence of discipleship.

Jesus chose twelve that they might **be** with Him. Yes, He counseled them, and He gave them certain supernatural gifts, but the core of their discipleship was to **be with Jesus** because He had won their hearts. In exactly the same way, you must invite your budding disciples to **be with you**.

You can't just pack your children off to a Christian day school and hope that they will learn to follow Jesus. Taking them to Sunday school and/or worship services and establishing family worship are only part of the answer. The main answer to what your children will become as they grow up stares back at you from your mirror every morning.

My daughters share some of my physical features (with the difference that on them it looks good). They also share a lot of my likes (Louis L'Amour books, Bing Crosby, old-time radio shows) and dislikes (bureaucrats, books by Charles Dickens, Cher). More importantly, they have also inherited many of their mother's and my beliefs and convictions in the form of a Biblical world-and-life view.

What we share in common with our children came about first as a result of winning their hearts (through high control -- child discipline -- and high support) and then as the fruit of days, months and years of time spent in the course of daily living. The Bible gives us a picture of exactly this kind of discipling.

> *Hear, O Israel, the LORD our God is one LORD: and thou shalt love the LORD thy God with all thine heart, and with all thy soul, and with all thy might. And these words, which I command thee this day, shall be in thine heart: and thou shalt*

teach them diligently unto thy children, and shalt talk of them when thou walkest by the way, and when thou liest down, and when thou risest up (Deuteronomy 6:4-7).

This passage tells us that Israel received a command to love God supremely. Not only was this love to fill their own hearts, but God gave them the responsibility to teach it to their children. They had to teach not just the words *about* loving God, but *actually to love Him.* You don't learn this kind of lesson in a lecture or an organized class. You learn it in the course of life. And that's where you'll teach it to your children.

You must teach your children in and through the daily affairs of life, because the Christian life is personal. Our God is a personal God. Therefore Christianity is more than a collection of impersonal facts. You can make your children memorize[56] the catechism and many scripture verses, but just having the words in their memory does not guarantee that they can understand or apply them in practice.

I have seen families where memorization of Scripture becomes a point of pride with the parents. "See how many verses Suzy can recite?" Then five minutes later Suzy is inflicting some hideous cruelty on a companion. What good has her memorization done her? You want your children not only to know the words, but to understand and live them as well. This is best learned by showing as well as telling.

Don't ever kid yourself. Dad, when your eyes linger on the woman walking by ... or when your speed exceeds

---

[56]I believe in a certain amount of memorization, **but** if I had to make the choice between my child's understanding a passage of Scripture and being able to recite it perfectly, I'd opt for understanding.

the legal limit (until you see the police car), you are teaching your children by your hypocrisy. In the same way, when you return the five-dollar bill to the store where the clerk had mistakenly given it to you instead of a one, or you help the elderly lady struggling with her packages, the youngsters will learn both your Biblical worldview and the lifestyle which grows out of it.

As you experience the affairs of life together, talk about them. I don't mean that you need to lecture or preach. Just use the occasion to have a quiet discussion about the meaning of the event you and your child have shared. Don't try to make an object lesson out of everything, though, and don't worry if you don't have Bible verses on the tip of your tongue for each occasion. Just communicate your Christian worldview in the midst of family living.

Of course, this presupposes that you already have a Christian worldview. Many people assume that because they are Christians, their view of life and what it's all about is Christian as well. For most of us, however, the development of a truly Christian worldview has taken much study and work. And this side of heaven, the work and study are never really complete.

2. God's Word: The Answer Book

What is a worldview? It's a comprehensive view of all the world and what makes it tick. When I speak of a *Biblical* worldview, I mean an approach to life that judges everything you know about people, science, art, philosophy, history, politics, current events, etc., by Scripture. If you are a Christian with a Biblical Worldview, you treat the Bible as the foundation for everything you know.

134

The Christian school movement and the homeschool movement led to a rise in awareness of how your worldview affects everything you think, say and do. This led to a hunger, especially on the part of homeschool parents for printed materials dealing with how to apply the Christian worldview to the different branches of the curriculum. Many of those parents realized the danger posed by the humanism of the public school system, and they wanted to shield their children from it.

In the process of studying in order to teach their children the truth and to protect them from falsehood, they discovered something. They found to what an extent the humanistic worldview they encountered in their own public school days had affected their beliefs and thought processes. Thus, as they taught their children, they themselves began to learn to view all things from the perspective of Scripture.

These pioneer efforts are far from complete. Nevertheless, the progress is real, and if you are not a *worldview Christian*[57] I urge you to investigate the matter for your own sake and your children's. After all, the Book of Proverbs places a high premium on godly wisdom and understanding. This means learning to see everything from God's viewpoint as revealed in Holy Writ.

To develop a Biblical worldview you don't need to start from ground zero with nothing but your Bible and the world around you (which could be done, but it would leave no time for anything else). As an alternative I have placed a recommended reading list at the end of this chapter. In order to direct your children to a godly

---

[57] A worldview Christian is nothing more than a Christian who strives to keep his thoughts and opinions consistent with the teachings of Scripture.

mindset, you must develop one yourself, and a large part of that involves reading. So, if you aren't an avid reader yet, you should plan on becoming one.

A lot of dads tell me they try to read, but it puts them to sleep. That's sad, because God's people have always been a people of the Book. If you have some roadblock to reading[58], then get your spouse to read to you. How ever you do it, find some way around this problem, because you really need to set an example for your children as one who examines all of life in the light of a Christian worldview.

3. It Takes One to Teach One

You will serve as the template for your child's growth and discipleship. That means that whatever lacks in your own spiritual life will probably show up as a deficiency in his as well. However, if you are making serious efforts in the areas of your weakness, your offspring will notice and try to grow in the same departments also.

You might expect that since I'm writing this book, that I must think that I'm the perfect parent. Nothing could be further from the truth. I have confronted in my children such things as a short temper, lack of initiative or problems accepting responsibility. As I searched for ways to help them past these faults, I often discovered that they were simply reflecting back my own faults to me. So ... how did I manage to bring up four godly, industrious, responsible daughters? Well, for one thing, I married a godly, industrious, responsible [and **patient**] woman, but there's one thing more.

---

[58] Of course if reading puts you to sleep, you'll be snoozing long before you get to this page.

I once had a discussion with one of my adult daughters about what made the difference in how she and her sisters have turned out. She said that one thing stood out to her -- her parents' honesty. In other words, that we didn't pretend to be better than we were. When one of us made a mistake, we tried to admit it. When we sinned, we confessed it, and tried to correct it.

The fact is, as a Christian I still haven't arrived. And I'm not so stupid as to think that I can hide my flaws from my family. But, like you, I'm working on my shortcomings, and my wife and children know that, too. The point is, you don't have to be perfect to disciple your children. But if you pretend that you're perfect, they'll be on to your game in a flash.

In fact, it's good for your family to see you battle to overcome sin in your life. They are struggling with some of the same difficulties, and they will draw encouragement and inspiration from your example. Also, if you ask them to pray that you might make progress against your fears or your wrong attitudes or the tendency to gossip, complain, get angry, or whatever, then they will be more likely to ask you to pray about their problems.

At this point you may be saying, "This chapter is supposed to be about discipling my children, but so far all you've talked about is me and how I need to change." That's true, but I hope I have made it plain that in order to lead your children, you need to be setting the example. The Apostle Paul put it this way:
Be ye followers of me, even as I also am of Christ
(I Corinthians 11:1).
In order to lead your family you need to be ahead of them and going in the right direction. But you don't need to be *far* ahead. After all, to a kindergarten student second graders seem quite smart and grown

up. Your children will look up to you in the same way. BUT you must follow Christ so that you *stay ahead.* Then you may say, "Do as I say *and* as I do." And then you will be more able to carry out effectively another great task of discipling: giving wise counsel. And that is the topic of the next section.

4. Advice is Cheap; *Good* Advice, However...

In his retirement, my father-in-law started a strawberry farm. In order to do it right, he went to someone already in the business who also served as a consultant. My father-in-law paid $500 per hour in order to visit the operation, ask questions and learn all he could about raising strawberries. The money he spent on the consultant made the difference between success and failure his first year.

Good advice does not come cheaply. The one able to give it often pays dearly for the experience. The great tragedy is that those who need it most often want to hear advice the least. Your children will not fall into this category if you have done two things.

First, your children will listen to your words of counsel if you have faithfully used the rod to discipline them. The rod eventually drives out foolishness and leaves them open to wise teaching. Then you will no longer need the fear of the rod to control them, for,

> A reproof entereth more into a wise man than an hundred stripes into a fool (Proverbs 17:10).

At this stage your children will *want* to do right. I found my own children so ready to adopt my wife's and my standards that I had to be careful not to make a word of reproof too strong. For when they realized they had done wrong, they could be much harder on chastising themselves than I ever would.

You must also do something else if you want your children to heed your counsel. You need to develop the skills of a counselor. In this part of your Christian growth, as in others, you are following the Lord Jesus, for He is the Wonderful Counselor (Isaiah 9:6). Of course your own growth in Christ coupled with practical experience will help you to develop insight as your children's counselor. I want to recommend something else that will help you in becoming competent to counsel your offspring.

Jay Adams'[59] first book, *Competent to Counsel* will provide you with a good foundation for using the Bible to help your children as they grow. I would also recommend his book, *Helping People Change.* Dr. Adams operates on the presupposition that the Bible rather than psychology holds the key to helping people to solve their problems (I have listed both books at the end of the chapter).

While we are on the subject of solving problems, my advice to all the fathers reading this book is that you try to become a problem solver in the eyes of your children. Put the wheels back on your son's toy car and the head back on your daughter's doll. Then keep on helping them with their problems.

Sure, there will be toys you won't be able to fix, but try anyway. If your children know that you always make an effort to help, and if you are successful at least part of the time, they'll keep coming back, not just with broken toys, but with projects they want to do. You will be able to advise them on where to get more information, what tools and materials they'll need, etc.

---

[59] Jay Adams is to the modern Nouthetic or Biblical counseling movement what Moses was to Israel.

The most important aspect of this strategy is that it gets your children to come to you from a young age, with little problems you can solve. Then it keeps them coming back, as the years pass. And they'll come in the confidence that you care about what they are doing and that you will give their needs your undivided attention. I am convinced that the greatest gift that you can give your child at any stage of his development is your attention.

At one point I wanted to reinforce the idea to my children that they could come to me with their problems. So I asked them if there was any problem I could help them with. One of my daughters said she had trouble remembering to read her Bible daily. I told her I would think about it and get back to her. I said that because I didn't have a clue as to what to tell her.

As often happens with "great" ideas, it did not come while I was intensely thinking about it. It just popped into my mind later. "Duct tape!" My daughter and I made a large "B" (for *Bible*) out of duct tape on her bedroom door. I said, "Will you promise me that when you see this "B" as you go to bed, if you haven't read your Bible that day, you'll read it before you go to sleep?" She agreed, and when I checked back on her in a couple of days, she said it was working.

Now I realize that wasn't a very complex problem. And a more clever person would have thought of some kind of reminder right away. But my point is, if you start thinking of yourself as a problem solver, you might uncover some wellspring of creativity that you did not know you had. You could also become your children's Advisor of Choice for any question or problem they might have. And once they elect you to that exalted post, you will not likely ever have to worry about impeachment.

5. And While We're on the Subject...

As long as you're considering making yourself your children's chief advisor, it's a small step from there to becoming their full-time teacher as well. I'm talking about home schooling, or as I prefer to call it, home *education* (home ed). There's no doubt that the decision to educate your children at home will cost you something. On the other hand, I know of no other single thing that will enrich your family life as much as teaching your own children at home.

Since most of the time it's Mom who stays home to oversee a home ed program, I'll be talking specifically to her right now[60]. Probably the one thing that keeps most people from educating their own children at home is **fear**. You fear what family and friends might think, what the school district officials might say, or even that you might not succeed as a teacher.

The first two matters are spiritual problems that involve fearing men more than you love and care for your child. You'll have to work that out between yourself and the Lord. I'd like to say something about the third fear, though.

Probably the scariest thought for a new home ed mom is teaching her youngster to read. I want you to know that teaching reading actually involves a lot fewer skills than teaching a new language -- something you've already done if you have a toddler. Think about it for a moment.

When you brought your new baby home for the first time, it could only cry and perhaps make a few other

---

[60]Dad does need to be involved, though, and to support the effort fully.

sounds. From that first day you began to teach him to differentiate voices from other sounds. You also taught him to isolate speech sounds from the many noises a baby makes. Then you taught your child to put these sounds together into words, probably starting with "dada" and "mama".

After a time, you expanded your little one's vocabulary enough to start him speaking sentences. In order for junior to speak an intelligible sentence, you needed to teach him the basics of grammar and sentence structure. You probably did all this without a degree in linguistics or even a manual to follow. Admit it: you're a fantastic teacher!

Compared to teaching a whole language from scratch, teaching a child to read is a snap. But to allay your fears further, let me assure you that there are also some really great curriculum materials available to home ed parents. But there's an oft-ignored secret to education that will help you in teaching your child anything from the ABC's to advanced mathematics. The secret is *readiness.*

Children cannot do anything until they have developed physically and mentally to the point that they are ready. If your child spoke his first word a few months later than your best friend's baby, it was no big deal. Different children of comparable intelligence often develop at widely differing rates. Yet, when we put all these highly individualized children into a classroom, we expect them to develop and learn in lock-step -- at exactly the same pace.

As an example, take my own children. One of my daughters learned to read at the age of three. Another did not really put it all together until she was about six. They have both been bright and well-above-average students. What a mistake we would have made if we had tried to force one into the mold of the other.

According to one educational professional and home ed advocate[61], boys tend to mature less quickly than girls. Some perfectly normal, bright lads will not be ready to learn reading until age nine *or later.* The interesting thing about these late-bloomers is that once they are ready to read, they will normally catch up to their grade-level in less than a year -- if they have not been discouraged by those who pushed them too early.

Knowing that, answer this question: *Who will serve your child's needs better, an institutional school with twenty or more students per teacher, or you?* Even if you have six or seven children you will be able to offer more individual instruction to your child than the average teacher. Now answer another question: *Who will know your child and his individual needs and abilities better, the teacher who has him for one year, or you, the parent that has lived with him since he was born?* I hope you can begin to see some of the many advantages of educating your own children.

One of the most satisfying elements of home ed to me is to see my children develop a lifelong love of learning. So many people watch their children grow into toddlerhood filled with a probing curiosity that prompts a question that always begins, "Mommy, why...?" Then Mommy sends them to school.

Within a year or two, any time the child encounters something that might remotely resemble learning, he

---

[61] Raymond S. Moore & Dorothy N. Moore, *Better Late Than Early: A New Approach to Your Child's Education*, Reader's Digest Press, Washougal WA, 1986.

rejects it as boring. It's sad to see seven and eight year old children burned out by the institutionalized schooling process. When my wife and I began to do home ed, it took two full years outside of institutionalized education before the excitement of learning began to rekindle its light in the girls' eyes.

Then education became, for us, not so much a matter of following a detailed curriculum, but just keeping up with our children's interests. And of course, providing them with learning materials and opportunities. I have a daughter whose interests led her into all kinds of needlework. She taught herself to crochet, knit, and embroider (and to do needlepoint, if memory serves).

At one point she cultivated cotton and flax in a small plot in our back yard. She experimented with hand-spinning wool into yarn. She even spun some dog hair into a piece of yarn long enough to make a couple of rows in a scarf she knitted for the dog's owner.

She has served as a marvelous resource for her sisters, teaching them whatever of these skills they wanted to know. She and her sisters have similarly extended themselves into various areas of science, literature, home economics and the social "sciences" to pursue their interests far beyond what a mere school experience would have taught them. Nor have they found this approach a hindrance to entering college.

If, for some reason you decide not to home ed your children, let me offer one more piece of advice on the matter (okay, two pieces). First, I beg you not to send your children into the public school system. They claim to be neutral, so they teach all about math, science, history and so forth without any reference to God.

Just by leaving Him out, however, they communicate the primary lesson of humanism -- the idea that God and His Word are not necessary to life in this world. This stands in direct opposition to the Christian worldview we discussed earlier. Do you think you can compete with the public school that has your child thirty hours a week (plus homework and time on the school bus)? Not likely.

Second, if you decide to put your child in an institutional setting by enrolling him in a Christian day school, there's something I'd like you to do first. Please read *Back to the Blackboard* by Jay Adams (see list at end of chapter). It will aid you in choosing a good Christian school.

6. Of Standards and Rules

Sometimes my children have encountered people who take pity on them for all the rules they have to follow about what their mother and I forbid and allow. They find it hard to believe when one or another of my daughters informs them that there are no such rules. But it's true -- we don't operate our home on the basis of a long list of do's and don'ts.

Sure, the youngsters have assigned chores, and there's structure in the day with family devotions, study time and regular mealtimes. We just never burdened our children with all the rules that some parents feel are so important. As far as I'm concerned, such a practice just turns non-issues into points of contention. Take mealtimes, for instance.

I never could understand parents who require their children to eat a certain prescribed quantity of food. "You're going to sit at that table until tomorrow morning, if that's how long it takes for you to finish your plate."

Why is this a point of contention? If the child does not eat much for supper, he will probably be ready to eat at breakfast.

If the child's lack of interest in food actually threatens his health (a very rare situation), then he needs medical attention, not a daily bout with Dad over how much food he has consumed. A normally healthy child may not be hungry at mealtimes for a number of reasons, including between-meal snacks. But if you provide him with healthy and nutritious foods at snack time, why make yourself and the child miserable by force-feeding him at mealtimes?

If my child comes to the table without an appetite, I find it a much more pleasant solution to offer a glass of juice or milk and let her sit at the table. She can participate in the fellowship around the table without pressure from me or my wife. Then, just to **prove** I'm not uptight, I'll ask her if she couldn't eat just a bite of dessert.

One time at a church function someone asked about some food my daughter might dislike. To which one of the ladies replied, "At their house, they're not **allowed** to have likes and dislikes." I guess when you have strong convictions and you hold to them, people assume you rule with an iron fist. But, as I said, around our house it just isn't like that.

On one occasion the pastor of the church we attended took the youth to a theme park. They all rode in the same van with the pastor at the wheel. On the way home, these young people were discussing how close they would come to getting home by the time of their curfews. Only one youngster in the van did not have a curfew -- my daughter.

After all, the pastor was leading the group as well as driving, The children were in responsible hands and in good company. If they'd had car trouble or some other providential hindrance, I would have expected a phone call. So, what is the big deal about dictating an exact time of arrival? I'm far more concerned that as long as she is in the company of Christian people involved in a wholesome activity that she should **have a good time**.

One reason I believe we have not had to worry about using rules to impose our standards on our children is that very early our daughters accepted the standards of my wife and me. We never had to sit a teenager down to deliver a lecture on "Just say no to drugs." Laura and I don't use drugs, and the examples of drug use in the media and literature seemed to repel rather than entice our children. And from what we previously observed about child-training in Galatians three and four, this is what we should expect.

> Wherefore the law was our schoolmaster to bring us unto Christ that we might be justified by faith (3:24).

> Now I say, That the heir, as long as he is a child, differeth nothing from a servant, though he is lord of all; But is under tutors and governors until the time appointed of the father. (4:1-2).

The schoolmaster or pedagogue speaks of law or control (maintained by the discipline of the rod) that brings a child to Christ. During this period even a covenant child is in servitude until the time determined by his father.

The Christian father must discern the peaceable fruit of righteousness as it becomes evident in his child. Then he can relax control, knowing that the Holy Spirit has brought his son or daughter to a state of voluntary compliance. At this stage the child does not need the external control imposed by a long list of rules, but needs, rather, some guidance and practice in applying his parents' Biblical standards to the situations of his life. As this chapter suggests, he can best learn this by observation and participation in the life of his family.

Reading List

Worldview:
The Dominion Covenant: Genesis. Gary North, Institute for Christian Economics, Tyler TX,1982, 1987 -- It's not just about economics, but covers how the first truths of the first book of the Bible affect our thinking in many areas. This and many other Christian books are available online at www.freebooks.com. The site is a gold mine of Christian world-and-life-view material if you have Internet access, **all for free**. Check it out today. For printed copies of Dr. North's books contact:

Christian Liberty Press
502 West Euclid Ave.
Arlington Heights, IL 60004
phone: (847) 259-4444 Press 6
email: custserv@christianlibertypress.com
http://ebiz.netopia.com/clpress/shopsaltlightbooks/

Counseling:
Competent to Counsel: Introduction to Nouthetic Counseling. Jay E. Adams, Zondervan, Grand Rapids, 1970 -- This book is **the classic** introduction to truly *Biblical* or *Nouthetic counseling*. You'll find no warmed-over secular-humanist psychobabble here.

How to Help People Change: The Four-Step Biblical Process. Jay E. Adams, Zondervan, Grand Rapids,1986 -- Although oriented toward pastoral counseling, the principles are easily adapted to the home. Much helpful material necessary to discipling. These books and others by Dr. Adams can be ordered from Timeless Texts:

88261 Highway 73, Suite B
Stanley, NC 28164
phone: 800.814.1045, e-mail: info@timelesstexts.com
website: www.timelesstexts.com

Education:

Back to the Blackboard. Jay E. Adams, Presbyterian and Reformed Publishing Co., Phillipsburg, NJ, 1982 -- A must-read for anyone in any aspect of Christian education. For ordering information, see Timeless Texts, above.

The Philosophy of the Christian Curriculum. Rousas John Rushdoony, Ross House Books, Vallecito, CA, 1985. --You can find out about a Christian approach to every school subject in this one volume. For information on ordering this and many other Christian worldview books, contact:

> Ross House Books
> PO Box 67
> Vallecito, CA, 95251

Christian Book Distributors. CBD offers many resource books and how-to books for home ed families. You can visit their website at www.Christianbook.com. Or to receive their **free** catalog, call or write:

> Christian Book Distributors
> PO Box 7000
> Peabody, MA 01961-7000
> 1-800-247-4794

Christian Liberty Academy. CLA provides home ed families with a complete program including curriculum, testing, etc.

> Christian Liberty Academy School System
> 502 W Euclid Avenue
> Arlington Heights IL 60004-5495
> email: custserv@homeschools.org
> www.class-homeschools.org/index.html

Appendix:

Signs and Seals of the Covenant

I have purposely avoided this topic in the text of my book, because the controversy might turn off some readers and therefore deprive them of blessing and help they might otherwise receive. I include it in this appendix on a take-it-or-leave-it basis, knowing that if you're not ready for this teaching, there is no profit in belaboring the point.

The point is this: if covenant children are such as make up the kingdom of God; if they belong to Christ; if the Biblical position is to see and treat them as *babes in Christ,* then they should receive the covenant sign and seal of baptism.

Under the Mosaic Covenant, male covenant children received the sign of circumcision because the promises of covenant succession made that covenant *trans-generational* in nature. Since the New Covenant like-wise contains promises of covenant succession (Acts 2:39, *et. al.*), we should extend the covenant sign to our children. The big question here is, did God extend more grace to children under the Mosaic Covenant than He does in Christ?

A related question here is the admission of very young children to the Communion table. For an answer to this question I direct the reader to the following book:

Feed My Lambs by Tim Gallant (Pactum Reformanda Publishing, Box 23009, Grande Prairie AB, Canada T8V 6X2.)

150

Printed in the United States
19552LVS00008B/22